THE
AMERICAN REVOLUTION:
A Constitutional Interpretation

BY

CHARLES HOWARD McILWAIN

GREAT SEAL BOOKS

A Division of Cornell University Press

ITHACA, NEW YORK

To

MY FATHER AND MOTHER

". . . di tutte le servitu dure quella e durissima che ti sottomette ad una Republica." Machiavelli, *Discorsi sopra la Prima Deca di T. Livio.*

PREFACE

This little book was finished before *Political Ideas of the American Revolution,* by Professor Randolph Greenfield Adams (Durham, N. C., 1922), came into my hands, hence this is my only opportunity of expressing my pleasure at the corroboration of the views set forth here by the work of another student who has reached the same general conclusion from another starting point and by a wholly different path. Professor Adams's point of view is political; that of this essay is constitutional. I have dealt mainly with precedents; he was largely concerned with contemporary American statements of the imperial problem of the eighteenth century, and the fullness and adequacy of his treatment of the latter make me very glad I decided originally not to take them up in detail. As it happens, therefore, we have traversed ground almost entirely different, and our minor deductions vary widely; but, I take it, our main conclusions are practically identical: that the central problem of the American Revolution was the true constitution of the Empire.

I am aware, of course, that by some it is regarded as wholly idle to discuss the constitutional issues involved in the American Revolution from any point of view. Independence was inevitable if not foreordained. Had it not occurred when it did and as it did, it must have come sooner or later in some way or other. The forces of nationalism were making it inevitable long before 1774 and it is a waste of time to try to discover the particular constitutional issues on which the actual breach happened to be made. In answer to such a view, while conscious of the great importance of the nationalistic forces in our history, I can only say in general that for the "inevitable" character of historical events as a theory I have not the very highest regard; and, more specifically, that of nationalistic characteristics in the thirteen colonies making independence "inevitable" in 1774, I can see few that do not seem equally discoverable in Upper Canada about 1837. "Inevitable" results in history, like exclusively racial explanations of it, are about the last resort of the despairing historian.

Discussions with my colleagues, Professor Wilbur C. Abbott and Dr. Frederick Merk on the topics treated here have been of great service in clarifying

my ideas about them, and in addition I am greatly indebted to Dr. Merk and to my wife for valuable sug-
gestions as to the form and manner of treatment to be
followed.

Cambridge, Mass.

C. H. McILWAIN

CONTENTS

CHAPTER I

INTRODUCTORY—THE PROBLEM

THE American Revolution began and ended with the political act or acts by which British sovereignty over the thirteen English colonies in North America was definitely repudiated. All else was nothing but cause or effect of this act. Of the causes, some were economic, some social, others constitutional. But the Revolution itself was none of these; not social, nor economic, nor even constitutional; it was a political act, and such an act cannot be both constitutional and revolutionary; the terms are mutually exclusive. So long as American opposition to alleged grievances was constitutional it was in no sense revolutionary. The moment it became revolutionary it ceased to be constitutional. When was that moment reached? The Americans stoutly insisted during the whole of their contest with Parliament to the summer of 1776 that their resistance was a constitutional resistance to un-constitutional acts. If their claim was justified the American Revolution can hardly be said to have occurred much before May, 1776. For it was the basis of the contemporary American contention that Parliament could constitutionally pass no act affecting the internal polity of the colonies, and hence no colonial opposition to such acts could be revolutionary. Only when the opposition was turned against an authority that was constitutional could this opposition be truly revolutionary; and for the Americans there was but one such authority, not the Parliament but the Crown. For them, therefore, the struggle continued to be merely a constitutional struggle for the recovery of legal rights and the redress of illegal wrongs up to the point where the power of the Crown was touched. The basis of their contention was a clear-cut distinction between the King in Parliament and the King out of Parliament, and so late as October 26, 1774, they solemnly assured George III that they wished "not a diminution of the prerogative." [1]

On the other hand it can scarcely be expected that English statesmen who had declared in the solemn form of a statute that the English Parliament "had,

---

[1] *Journals of the Continental Congress*, edited by Ford, vol. 1, p. 119.

hath, and of right ought to have" sufficient power and
authority to bind the American colonies, subjects of
the Crown of Great Britain in all cases whatsoever,
would regard American opposition to Parliament's
practical application of this power in such statutes as
the Massachusetts Government Act as a merely "constitutional" opposition, or their resistance to its enforcement as anything less than revolutionary. For
these English statesmen, the Revolution of 1688-9 had
ended the older sharp distinction between the King
in Parliament and the King out of Parliament. Prerogative had become for them only such part of the
ancient discretionary right of the Crown as Parliament saw fit to leave untouched. All rights of the
Crown in the dominions, as well as in the Realm,
were now completely under the control of Parliament,
since William and Mary had sworn in their coronation oath to govern the Kingdom "and the dominions
thereunto belonging according to the statutes in Parliament agreed on."

On this interpretation it is obvious that the acts of
the Americans had ceased to be constitutional and
became revolutionary in character long before they
ceased to protest their loyalty to the "best of Kings."
They must be considered so from the first time the
power of Parliament constitutionally to bind the

colonies was definitely denied.   This occurred long
before 1776.

The bare statement of these two inconsistent and
conflicting views at once suggests the first constitutional problem.   When did the first revolutionary act
occur?   What is the date of the American Revolution?   Is it coincident with the first definite breach of
the royal prerogative, or should it be found in the
earlier repudiation of Parliament's authority?   No
answer can possibly be made to this important question
one way or the other till the conflicting constitutional
views of the Americans and the English Parliament
are carefully compared and some conclusion reached
on their respective merits; and this conclusion itself
must be based upon the constitutional precedents to be
found in the whole historical development of the English constitution up to the time of the American
struggle.

When did the train of constitutional development
begin which led in continuous sequence to the first act
that may be called revolutionary?   Who were the real
adversaries in this constitutional struggle, and which
of them was constitutionally "right"?   These are a few
of the questions that occur to one who attempts to
make a general survey of this period.   The answers
they have received are singularly contradictory and

frequently unconvincing, and this after all the pains-
taking research of recent years. The purpose of this
brief study is to try if possible to narrow these constitutional questions until they become susceptible of
clear and definite treatment, if not of conclusive answers. We shall not be concerned with the intricate
network of "causes," economic, social, or political, tremendous as is the importance of them all. They
must be at the background of our minds, not the fore-
ground.

Thus stripped of its constitutional non-essentials the
American Revolution seems to have been the outcome
of a collision of two mutually incompatible interpretations of the British constitution, one held by the subjects of the British King in America, the other by a
majority in the British Parliament. This result was a
breach of the constitution not based upon and not
warranted by the earlier precedents in the constitution's
growth. On an examination of this constitutional
struggle that brought on the Revolution, I find myself
unavoidably at variance with many of the views that
seem at the present day to be becoming canonical,
especially among American historians.

The struggle popularly called the American Revolution, up to its latest constitutional phase, was a contest
solely between the Americans and Parliament. The

Crown was not involved. No question of prerogative was at issue. If the King was at all implicated, it was the King in Parliament only and as a constituent part thereof, not the King in Council. The struggle did not touch the prerogative till after George III's Proclamation of Rebellion of August 23, 1775, and in fact can hardly be safely dated earlier than the formal declaration of the Virginia Convention on June 29, 1776, that "the government of this country, as formerly exercised under the crown of Great Britain, is *totally dissolved*" [1] or Congress's resolution of May 15, 1776, recommending to the various colonies the adoption of popular constitutions, with its famous preamble which declares that "it appears absolutely irreconcileable to reason and good Conscience, for the people of these colonies now to take the oaths and affirmations necessary for the support of any government under the crown of Great Britain, and it is necessary that the exercise of every kind of authority under the said crown should be totally suppressed, and all the powers of government exerted, under the authority of the people of the colonies." [2]

---

[1] F. N. Thorpe, *The Federal and State Constitutions,* vol. vii, p. 3815.

[2] *Journals of the Continental Congress* (Ford), vol. iv, p. 358, "The preamble and the resolution, taken together, formed a

There can be no doubt of the revolutionary character of these declarations. Possibly some of the previous acts of the Congress and the colonies might be considered revolutionary, though it seems better to regard them up to that time as rebellious rather than revolutionary. A deliberate intent to establish permanent governments independent of the Crown must have existed before mere rebellion turned into revolution. Up to May, 1776, then, the American claims were aimed solely at the power of Parliament. About that time they first began to be directed against the Crown. As soon as they were so directed their revolutionary character becomes obvious. No American would then have denied that they were revolutionary, and no historian can now do so. This last phase of the controversy, this defiance of prerogative, however, began very late; in fact, not until many months after the constitutional struggle had turned into the civil war which we call from its final outcome the War of Independence. There might be a difference of opinion as to the relative merits of the American and the English claims of "right" in this final phase of the contest; but

---

statement of congressional conviction that the colonies were no longer parts of the British empire."

Edward Channing, *A History of the United States,* vol. iii, p. 199.

since it is admittedly a mere "right of revolution" that would be asserted or denied in such a discussion, it concerns the rights of man rather than the British constitution and has little place in a treatment strictly constitutional.

But what of the earlier phase, by far the larger phase, when American opposition is aimed solely at Parliament?   Is that too revolutionary?   Or is it merely constitutional?   Did the American Revolution begin about 1761 or only with the attack on the Crown in 1776 ? This is a question harder to answer, and the answer must depend on matters purely constitutional, not political, as in the case of the defiance of the Crown after 1776.

For the period between 1761 and 1776 the non-revolutionary or revolutionary character of the resistance of the Americans must be judged upon the basis of the soundness or unsoundness of their constitutional claims.   For those who believed that the parliamentary acts of which they complained were but parts of a settled plan to deprive them of legal rights by unconstitutional means, it might even seem a question whether the revolutionary acts were not up to 1776 all on the side of a Parliament that had assumed and exercised a power for which there was no warrant in English constitutional precedent.   Long before that, they might plausibly have argued, the "unconstitutional" acts of the British Parliament itself had assumed a character nothing less than revolutionary, though it might be difficult to fix the exact point of time when they could first be said to be revolutionary as well as unconstitutional. On the latter supposition why might not the American Revolution properly enough be said to begin as early as May, 1649, with the Act that established the Commonwealth, with supreme authority in the Parliament of the English people over "the dominions thereunto belonging," apparently the first formal assertion by a Parliament of its authority beyond the realm?

It is conceded by historians of all shades of opinion that the English Revolution of 1688-9 was a real revolution. The unprecedented events of those years definitely placed the power of Parliament above the royal prerogative and gave to the modern limited monarchy in England its unique constitutional character. All admit this. What was in 1689 revolutionary was accepted in England as subsequently constitutional and legitimate for the realm and "the dominions thereunto belonging," on the theory of Locke that a people can change its constitution through the right of revolution. Englishmen in England had acquiesced in it. But what of "the dominions thereunto belonging"? Acts originally admittedly revolutionary could there only become legitimate by acquiescence and consent too. Had the "dominions" consented when they acclaimed the new sovereigns sworn under the new coronation oath to govern "according to the statutes in Parliament agreed on"? Or was the consent of the dominions immaterial when the realm alone had legitimated the new régime? Were the dominions concluded by the acts of Englishmen in the realm alone? Samuel Adams and Governor Hutchinson in 1773 seemed to see this constitutional issue more clearly than many subsequent historians. It was Adams's primary contention that what was revolutionary in 1688 remained revolutionary until assented to, that it had not been consciously assented to in America, and that therefore it was revolutionary in 1773 for the dominions as it had been in the realm in 1688. One of Hutchinson's main contentions was that America had given its assent as fully as England had when the usurping William and Mary had been proclaimed in the colonies. Adams was demanding that the stream of precedents for parliamentary control of the colonies should be followed up further towards its source, that the revolution of 1688 should be allowed to break the continuous validity of precedent only if it was acquiesced in by all those affected; in short, that revolution only becomes a basis for legitimate government when accepted by a people, and that one people cannot accept for another. His views imply that England and the colonies are *not* "one people." To his mind America had not accepted, and on true political principles England could not accept for her. Hence the power of Parliament, new and revolutionary in England in 1688, was for the dominions revolutionary still in 1773. He held that the issue should in 1773 still be settled on the lines of the constitution as it existed before 1689, and that that constitution gave no ground for the powers "usurped" by Parliament in the eighteenth century. In reality this was a collision of the older interpretation of the English Constitution, continuing in America, but superseded after 1689, if not 1649, in England, with the post-revolutionary interpretation as held in England. The relative merits of these two views depend on the question whether the colonies were bound to push their precedents back no further than the middle of the seventeenth century. This in turn depends upon whether they had consciously accepted the new basis for themselves after the accession of William and Mary or were concluded by the act of the people of England alone, entirely regardless of their own wishes and views.[1]

---

[1] John Adams, with his usual keenness, saw the importance of the question as to whether America had acquiesced in Parliament's authority, and denied it in the letters of *Novanglus.*

A final decision upon the whole question of America's acquiescence in all Parliament's earlier acts affecting her is one to be made only after a careful examination of all the facts, a question which should be examined more minutely than it has been.   Here, however, I can only indicate some of its theoretical aspects.

Commentators who are often more legalists than legists have, as it seems to me, been overfond of applying to the larger questions of constitutional development a too narrow and rigid interpretation based on superficial analogies drawn from other branches of

---

"The authority of parliament was never generally acknowledged in America." (Works of John Adams, iv, p. 47.) In proof he cites a number of protests against it in America (*ibid.,* p. 48). He said the Americans made a concession in imperial matters, but never in those of internal polity (p. 49). No duties were imposed for revenue before 1764, and these were immediately protested against (pp. 49-50). The act against slitting mills and tilt hammers was never enforced, the hatters act was never regarded (*ibid.*). Acts of trade alone have been acquiesced in practically as treaties of commerce (*ibid.,* 113-114). This was a voluntary cession of power (p. 130). By such a cession Parliament has authority in commerce, but no cession exists in internal matters, and there never was an acquiescence in such. If they were on the statute book, the Americans thought little of them, as they were either ignored or unenforced. In the rare cases where enforcement occurred immediate protest followed. In short, he holds that there is nothing to prove, and much to disprove, the assertions of *Massachusettensis* that America by her actions had acknowledged the authority of Parliament—except in matters of external trade, a point they were still willing in 1774 to concede in practice.

law, such as the law of property or of contract. The technicalities of the law of estoppel and of prescription and the statutory provisions extinguishing a civil remedy by lapse of time are thus used sometimes rather loosely and without discrimination to prove a whole people's forfeiture by non-user of its former right of opposition to unconstitutional grievances.

Such a commentator might be reminded that as early as the Twelve Tables prescription in a stolen article was forbidden; that neither provincial lands, nor *res sacrae* or *religiosae* were prescriptible at Roman law; that the adverse possession requisite for valid prescription even where it was applicable must be *nec vi, nec clam, nec precario*; that extinctive prescription was excluded by minority and other disabilities; and that even the law of slavery was tempered by the *jus postliminii*. He should be urged to note that the limitation of civil actions is not extended in our law to prosecutions for crime; and might be asked on what general reasoning he is warranted in restricting the principle of the maxim *nullum tempus occurrit regi*, under which this is justified, merely to a king instead of extending it generally to a people as well.

But after all it was public policy that first created prescription and public policy also imposed restrictions upon its operation, and technical considerations of the sort mentioned above whether used intelligently or not—and they have not always been used intelligently—have really little place in a discussion involving questions of the rights of subjects against rulers. Even conservatism might be expected to have some limits. Molyneux denied the fact of the conquest of Ireland, but he also denied that a right of permanent domination can ever be legitimately based on conquest. As Otis put it, "There can be no prescription old enough to supersede the law of nature."[1]

This is no question to be decided on mere legal analogy and that an uncritical one. I can see little legal, constitutional, or political ground for the assertion that the American colonists were forever estopped from resisting the application to them of an authority which they had come to believe to be unwarranted by precedent, merely because for a time the laxity of that application had led them and their ancestors to pay slight attention to the subject. And it certainly is a strange assumption, that the colonists in proclaiming William and Mary must inevitably have accepted and for all time all the unforeseen constitutional consequences that an oligarchical parliament might later

[1] Post, p. 154.

choose to deduce from the transactions of 1688 and
1689. How many Americans, presumably, were ac-
quainted with the form of the English coronation oath
in 1689?

The last question, it is true, belongs to political theory rather than to constitutional interpretation, and in
part turns on the mere question of fact whether or not
there was an actual conscious acquiescence in America
in the Revolution and in all its constitutional implica-
tions later accepted in England; but other questions
go much further than this. Samuel Adams's contention,
implied if not expressed, that the colonies are not concluded by the action of the realm alone really touches
one of the deepest problems in English constitutional
history. He brought into question, though not for
the first time in the Empire, the validity of the famous
pronouncement of Parliament of May 19, 1649, that
"the people of England and of all the dominions and
territories thereunto belonging are . . . a Commonwealth."

Upon the whole matter it has apparently become
the orthodox view among American historians that the
English were right and the Americans wrong, that
however wrong-headed, impolitic, or even oppressive
Parliament's treatment of America may have been, on
purely constitutional grounds the English case is the

better; that the letter of the law was on their side. We
are here not concerned either with policy or with eth-
ics. On its constitutional side this question narrows
down to the simple issue as to whether the American
or the English interpretation of the British constitution is the one more properly deducible from the precedents furnished by the development of that constitution in the whole period of its growth up to the
time of the struggle. The Americans denied the authority under English constitutional law of the Parliament at Westminster to bind Englishmen beyond
the realm. They also asserted that parts of that law
were wholly beyond Parliament's reach, were "fundamental," and that any act of Parliament in contraven-
tion of these parts was void. English statesmen asserted in reply that there was nothing beyond the
power of the English Parliament, whether in the
Realm or "in the Dominions thereunto belonging."
These are purely constitutional issues. I am concerned here with no other. They are questions to be
decided entirely on the basis of precedents. I propose
to examine these precedents, but at the risk of contradiction, for the sake of clearness, I shall anticipate the
discussion to express my belief that this question of
"right" or "wrong" if kept within strict constitutional
lines is susceptible of some answer; and, contrary to

the view that now seems current among American historians,[1] that that answer must on the whole be more favorable to the claims of the American colonists than to those of the British statesmen who opposed them in Parliament.

---

[1] The following extract from a recent book by a careful and competent American historian may serve as an example: "At best, an exposition of the political theories of the anti-parliamentary party is an account of their retreat from one strategic position to another. . . . Without discounting in any way the propagandist value attaching to popular shibboleths as such, it may as well be admitted that the colonists would have lost their case if the decision had turned upon an impartial consideration of the legal principles involved." *New Viewpoints in American History,* by Arthur Meier Schlesinger, Professor of History in the University of Iowa, New York, 1922, p. 179.

CHAPTER II

THE PRECEDENTS—THE REALM AND THE DOMINIONS

For clearness of treatment of the precedents underlying the constitutional claims set up by the Americans between 1765 and 1776 probably no better division of the subject could be found than the one contained in the declaration of the Continental Congress in 1774 in which the rights of the colonists are based on "the immutable laws of nature, the principles of the English constitution, and the several charters or compacts;"[1] though the chronological order of actual insistence upon these several claims from 1765 to 1776 was the inverse of that in the declaration. Adopting this classification I shall try to examine the earlier precedents for their claims, first, in the principles of the British constitution; secondly, in the colonial charters; and thirdly, in the law of nature. Of these, the third may be dismissed very summarily in a discussion that does not go beyond the constitutional, its chief importance being the question whether the law of na-

---

[1] *Journals of the Continental Congress,* ed. Ford i, 67.

ture is not "engrafted in the English constitution," as Camden said. Upon the second, for reasons both theoretical and practical, far less reliance was placed by the Americans than upon their rights as Englishmen. Upon the precedents for these rights of Englishmen, therefore, most of our discussion must centre, with briefer notice of such claims as were based on charters and natural rights.

Their rights as Englishmen were to the Americans the safest and surest ground of opposition to the Parliament. Upon these, therefore, they put their chief reliance and for their proof they offered their most elaborate arguments. For this reason these rights must be placed foremost and must receive the fullest attention in a modern discussion of the issues involved in the American Revolution.

But the assertion and the safeguarding of these rights of Englishmen of necessity drove the Americans to deny the prevailing English theory of the omnipotence of Parliament. It is important to note the two-fold character of this denial. On the one hand, the Americans contended that the competence of Parliament to make law was strictly limited to such laws only as affected those parts of the King's dominions from which parliamentary representatives were summoned. On the other hand, they held that there were certain fundamental rights which were inalienable, and could be neither altered, abridged, nor destroyed by any means whatsoever; they existed by the law of nature, which was a part of the British constitution. With Cicero the Americans considered them a part of that "true law conformable to right reason, shared in by all, constant and eternal . . . to change or detract from which divine law forbids."[1] An inalienable, indefeasible right, of which men cannot deprive themselves, is, of course, totally beyond the reach of any representative body, however perfect. Men can only delegate what they have, and they have no power directly or indirectly to alter or destroy these fundamental rights.

Of these two arguments the first is by far the more concrete and definite; for this reason the more susceptible of conclusive proof or disproof, and consequently much the stronger if proved. In fact, this argument, based solely in British precedent, that acts of the Parliament of England bind not the dominions of the King elsewhere, actually furnished the surest basis of the whole American contention and the chief reason for believing today that the American claims had a constitutional justification. To it, then, we

---

[1] *De Re Publica,* iii, 22.

must direct our first and fullest attention. To do so adequately, it will be necessary first to trace in brief the whole train of continuous constitutional development which led directly to the American struggle. This train of events, I believe, had a definite and discoverable beginning, and once begun, it led straight to revolution.

The series of constitutional developments to which I have just referred goes back further than is often suspected. Revolution occurred only in 1776, but the direct and continuous constitutional causes of it definitely began neither later nor earlier than May 19, 1649. On that day the Parliament passed the act establishing the Commonwealth, and in the following terms:

"Be it Declared and Enacted by this present Parliament and by the Authority of the same, That the People of England, and of all the Dominions and Teritories thereunto belonging, are and shall be, and are hereby Constituted, Made, Established, and Confirmed to be a Commonwealth and Free-State: And shall from henceforth be Governed as a Commonwealth and Free-State, by the Supreme Authority of this Nation, The Representatives of the People in Parliament, and by such as they shall appoint and constitute as Officers and Ministers under them for the

good of the People, and that without any King or
House of Lords"[1]

The direct constitutional antecedents of the American Revolution begin with this first formal adoption
of the fatal phrase "The People of England and all
the dominions and territories *thereunto belonging.*"
The startling statement is here for the first time officially made that the lands formerly the King's dominions outside the realm "are and shall be" the property
of *"The People of England,"* that though they are
outside the realm and have no representatives in its
Parliament they nevertheless are parts of *one* Commonwealth, henceforth to be governed "by the Supreme Authority *of this Nation,* the Representatives
of the People in Parliament."   The entire basis of
Parliament's claim in the Declaratory Act of 1766 is
here, a right to bind the colonies "in all cases whatsoever," and here it is formally asserted for the first
time.   This is the true beginning of the constitutional
issue that directly led to the Declaration of Independence, for this novel declaration, this tremendous in-
novation, includes all that the Americans protested
against from 1765 to 1776.   And it was an innova-
tion.   Its like cannot be found in any earlier official

---

[1] Firth and Rait, *Acts and Ordinances of the Interregnum,* ii, p.
122; also in Scobell, ii, 30; Gardiner, *Documents,* p. 297.

document. Here for the first time is found that disastrous political subordination to the Englishmen of
"this Nation" and to the "Supreme Authority" of
their parliament, of all other Englishmen outside the
realm in the other dominions formerly belonging to
the King. Its importance has not been sufficiently appreciated by historians of the United States or of the
British Empire.[1] To make clear this importance it

---

[1] John Dickinson in his *Essay on the Constitutional Power of
Great Britain over the Colonies in America,* in 1774, wrote: "A
dependence on the crown and Parliament of Great Britain is a
novelty—a dreadful novelty. It may be compared to the engine
invented by the Greeks for the destruction of Troy. It is full
of armed enemies, and the walls of the constitution must be
thrown down, before it can be introduced among us." He says
further: "This word 'dependence,' as applied to the states connected with England, seems to be a new one. It appears to have
been introduced into the language of the law, by the commonwealth act of 1650. A 'dependence on parliament' is still more
modern. A people cannot be too cautious in guarding against
such innovations" (p. 385).
A comparison of the act of 1649 with earlier statutes mentioning dominions beyond the realm fully justifies Dickinson's
assertion of the former's novel character. To take one example
only, in the preamble of Elizabeth's Act of Supremacy (1 Eliz.,
c. i, 1559), there is a reference to the "putting away of all
usurped and foreign powers and authorities out of this your
realm, and other your highness's dominions and countries." Such
language seems more naturally to imply equality than "dependence"; and these "dominions and countries" belong not to the
people, nor even to "the Crown," but alone to her "highness." It
is not even said that they belong to the Queen as such.
It is true that the very enactment in Parliament of this and

will be necessary to show (1) the antecedents of this act, (2) the earliest resistance to its central principle, (3) the historical and constitutional justification of this principle and of the objections made to it, and (4) the historical connection of this important act with the later part of the constitutional struggle in the American colonies.

The execution of Charles I only augmented, it did

---

other statutes of the Tudor period in regard to the royal supremacy or titles in ecclesiastical matters might seem to imply an authority to bind the dominions beyond the realm; but the wording of the acts themselves and especially of their preambles indicates that this was no more than an affirmance of a royal authority assumed (rightly or wrongly) to have existed from a time beyond legal memory in the right of the Crown alone. It carries with it no further implication of Parliament's legislative authority over outside dominions than the analogous affirmance of ancient customary law affecting matters other than "the estate of the King and his heirs."

Before 1542 the King of England had for Ireland merely the title of *Lord* (*Dominus*). By Proclamation of January 23, 1541-2 Henry VIII first assumed the title of King of Ireland, and on the request *of ,his subjects of Ireland* only, as he formally declares (*Tudor and Stuart Proclamations,* vol. i, No. 219; *Letters and Papers,* vol. xvii, No. 47). This request was contained in an Irish Statute, 33 Henry VIII, c. i. By the proclamation any omission of this new title was punishable from the last day of April, 1542; but not till 1543 was the new style ratified by act of the *English* Parliament, Statute 35 Henry VIII, c. iii, *An Act for the Ratification of the King's Majesty's Stile.* The nature of these events and the order of their sequence are not without significance for the question of the "dependence" of the "dominions and countries" out of the realm, and of all of them.

not create, the problem of government with which the
parliamentary leaders were confronted. Ever since
the Long Parliament's formal assumption of independent power in its Declaration of May 27, 1642,[1] it had
exercised powers that were wholly unprecedented and
entirely illegal, and even before that time many of its
acts in regard to Ireland, in the beginning though still
enacted in due form by King, Lords, and Commons,
were alleged by the Irish to be unprecedented and unconstitutional. With the death of the King the unconstitutionality of Parliament's acts became even more
obvious and it was further necessary to establish some
kind of a government to replace the King's. The first
act of this latter kind was one creating the Council of
State of 13 February, 1648-9, including a set of in-
structions the first of which enjoined the suppression
of all who should maintain Charles II's claim "to the
Crowne of England, or Ireland, Dominion of Wales,
or to any of the dominions or territoryes to them or
eyther of them belonging." [2] In another of these in-
structions, the Channel Islands and Man are spoken
of as "belonging to the Common-Wealth of England."
On March 17 was passed the act abolishing the office

---

[1] Rushworth, iv, 551.

[2] Firth and Rait, *Acts and Ordinances of the Interregnum*, vol.
ii, p. 3.

of King,[1] which also refers to "the people of England and Ireland and the Dominions and Territories thereunto belonging."

In these, and in all other occurrences of the phrase before 1649,[2] "belonging" seems to mean little more than "a part of." But in 1649 a new and more sinister meaning appears: the dominions become in reality "British possessions." Disastrous as this ultimately came to be, it is hard to see what else the parliament leaders could have done at that time. These outside dominions had belonged to the King. Now that a government without a King had been set up, only two alternatives seemed possible: to place them under the control of Parliament, or to renounce entirely all control over them. Obviously the former alone was feasible in 1649, and, of course, all its future results could not then have been foreseen. In a sense, then, it was the temporary abolition of kingship which created the constitutional issue from which in time the American Revolution resulted.

Before the middle of the sixteenth century Henry VIII's Statute of Appeals in 1532 had declared "that

---

[1] *Ibid.*, ii, p. 18.

[2] As, for example, the statute declaring the right of James I, to the Crown (Statute 1, James I, chapter i), "the imperial crown of the realm of England, and of all the kingdoms, dominions and rights belonging to the same."

this Realm of *England* is an Empire, and so hath been accepted in the World, governed by one supreme Head and King, having the Dignity and Royal Estate of the Imperial Crown of the same." [1] But it is there said that the realm itself is an Empire. Parliament was emphasizing only the realm of England's independence of Imperial and Papal authority. She claimed what Bartolus or Lupold von Bebenburg would have called *merum et mixtum imperium* and somewhat more; but it was only a claim of independent sovereignty for England, it was no claim to a power over other lands than England. With the Long Parliament the real problem of the modern British Empire first appears in definite form. Then for the first time, if we disregard a few earlier and much less definite transactions between the English Parliament and other dominions of the Crown in the later Middle Ages and just after, came in question in its modern form the constitutional relation of the realm and the dominions without, a question that still remains the central constitutional problem of the British Empire.

The actual employment of these new parliamentary powers in the Plantations was not long delayed. On October 3, 1650, an act was passed in Parliament

_____
[1] 24 Henry VIII, chapter xii.

prohibiting trade with Barbadoes, Virginia, and other plantations, with a preamble declaring that these have been and are "Colonies and Plantations, which were planted at the Cost, and settled by the People, and by Authority of this Nation, which are and ought to be subordinate to, and dependent upon England; and hath ever since the Planting thereof been, and ought to be subject to such Laws, Orders and Regulations as are or shall be made by the Parliament of England." [1]

On October 9th, 1651, was enacted the first of the series of Navigation Acts which played so important a part in creating the later hostility to the English Parliament in America.[2]

But actual legislation for the dominions had occurred earlier, and some ten years before this the Long Parliament had begun a series of acts for Ireland which gave rise to the first attack upon Parliament's competence to make laws binding "dependencies of the Crown" outside the realm. To this we must now turn, for it is the first appearance of the exact contention upon which the thirteen American

[1] Firth and Rait, *Acts and Ordinances of the Interregnum,* ii, p. 425.

[2] Firth and Rait, *Acts and Ordinances of the Interregnum,* ii, p. 559ff.

colonies mainly relied a century and a quarter later, and the significance of this remarkable parallel has in large measure escaped the notice of American historians.

The question of Ireland's constitutional relation to the Kingdom of England arose in acute form soon after the recall of the Earl of Strafford. The Irish House of Commons, no doubt influenced by the example of the English House, entered upon an examination of their constitutional grievances, and in 1641 in the course of it, with the consent of the Irish House of Lords, submitted a list of constitutional questions to the Lords Justices in Ireland. The first of these questions was "Whether the Subjects of this Kingdom [Ireland] be a Free People, and to be Governed only by the Common Laws of England, and Statutes of Force in this Kingdom?" [1] The judges in their answer to this important query were careful to avoid any direct statement regarding the power of the English Parliament to bind Ireland; and so, as Nalson relates it, "The *Commons* not being satisfied with these Sober and Calm Resolutions of the Judges, fell to Voting their own Sense, and to make Declarations of

---

[1] John Nalson, *An Impartial Collection of the Great Affairs of State,* ii, 573. The answer of the judges to this question is given in Nalson, ii, 576.

the Law upon their former Queries." [1] Their own declaration upon this first question was that "The Subjects of this his Majesties Kingdom of *Ireland,* are a
free People, and to be Governed only, according [to]
the Common Law of *England,* and Statutes made and
established *by Parliament in this Kingdom of Ireland,*
and according to the Lawful Customs, used in the
same." [2]

In a conference between the Irish Lords and Commons on June 9, 1641, incident to the Commons' adoption of this declaration, Patrick Darcy, Esquire, a
Catholic member of the House, by order of the Commons delivered an argument in support of the constitutional view set forth in the declaration. [3] This and
the declaration itself constitute the first definite statement of the central point of the American opposition

---

[1] *Ibid.,* ii, p. 584.

[2] *Ibid.,* ii, p. 584. (The italics are not in the original.)

[3] It was printed at Waterford in 1643 by Thomas Bourke, printer
to the Confederate Catholics of Ireland, with the title, *An Argument Delivered by Patricke Darcy, Esquire; by the Expresse
Order of the House of Commons in the Parliament of Ireland,*
9 *Iunii,* 1641, and reprinted by G. F. in Dublin, in 1764. See also,
*Essay on the Antiquity and Constitution of Parliaments in Ire-
land,* by Henry Joseph Monck Mason, new edition with an Introduction by Very Rev. John Canon O'Hanlon, Dublin, 1891, 55ff.,
and Introduction, p. 112ff; *Historical Review of the Legislative
Systems Operative in Ireland,* by the Right Hon. J. T. Ball,
London, 1889, p. 34ff.

more than a century later. Patrick Darcy deserves
a place in American constitutional history. His general position is made clear in the statement, "And for
the statutes of *England* generall statutes were received in this kingdome, some at one time, some at another, and all generall statutes by *Poynings* Act, *anno*
10 *Hen.* 7, but no other statute, or new introducting
law, untill the same be first received and enacted in
Parliament in this kingdome"[1] which he proceeds to
prove by precedents.

The Irish Rebellion which broke out a few months
later was the immediate cause of a striking practical
enforcement of the English Parliament's claims of a
legislative power over Ireland, which served to keep
alive the agitation on the constitutional question. One
of the last parliamentary acts of Charles I was his
assent on March 19, 1642 to *An Act for the reducing
of the Rebels in Ireland to their Obedience to his
Majesty and the Crown of England.*[2] This act provided among other things for further extensive con-
fiscation of the lands of the Irish and a new plantation. It was followed on July 14, 1643, after the de-

---

[1] Darcy's *Argument*, p. 70 (*Reprint of* 1764).
[2] 16 Charles I, chapter xxxiii. See also, Rushworth's *Collections,* iv, folios 556-558; Lords' Journals, iv, p. 607; R. Dunlop,
Ireland under the Commonwealth, i, cxx-cxxv.

parture of the King, by an Ordinance of Parliament *for the encouragement of Adventurers, to make new subscriptions for Towns, Cities, and Lands in Ireland.*[1] After the spirited protest of 1641 it is not strange that this new parliamentary interference with the internal polity of Ireland should draw out further Irish declarations of opposition.

Following the passage of the Act of Adventurers, the Confederate Catholics of Ireland drew up a protestation to be presented to the King's Commissioners at Trim on March 17, 1642,[2] in which they object to the encroachment of the English Parliament upon that of Ireland and to the declaration "that Ireland was bound by Statutes made in England, if named, contrary to the known Truth, and the Laws settled here for 400 years."[3] They complain "That whereas Ireland has a Parliament of its own, and no Statute made in England ought to bind in Ireland, unless there established by Parliament," the English have nevertheless passed the recent Statute of Adventurers.[4] That act, they further declare, "though forced on his Majesty,

[1] Firth and Rait, *Acts and Ordinances of the Interregnum,* i, 192.

[2] It was printed at Waterford by Thomas Bourke, printer to the Confederate Catholics. Extracts from it are given by Rushworth with the answers of the Protestants. Rushworth, *Collections,* iv., p. 385ff. (Should be 417.)

[3] Rushworth, iv. 390. (Should be 422.)

[4] *Ibid.,* 396-397.

and in itself unjust and void, yet continues of evil
consequence . . . which therefore, they protest
against, as an Act without precedent, against the
King's prerogative, and the fundamental laws of the
Kingdom." [1] It is interesting to note that the Protestants in their answers to these protests are careful to
make no flat denial of the constitutional claims. They
were in fact admitted by many Protestants as well as
by Catholics in Ireland. The Irish House of Lords
even in protesting their abhorrence of the Rebellion in
November, 1641, promise to suppress it only "in such
a way, as by the *Authority of the Parliament of this
Kingdom,* with the approbation of his Excellent
Majesty or of his Majesty's chief Governor or Governors of this Kingdom shall be thought most
effectual." [2]

In the meantime wide circulation had been given to
manuscript copies of a little anonymous book entitled
*A Declaration setting forth How, and by what Means,
the Laws and Statutes of England, from Time to
Time, came to be of Force in Ireland.* On complaint
to the Irish House of Lords of this book, the matter
was dealt with in both Houses of the Irish Parliament,
a committee was appointed, and the whole book was

---

[1] Wt. Harris, Hibernica, Part II, preface.
[2] Nalson, ii, 898. (The italics are not in the original.)

read through in both houses.[1] A prorogation put an end to the proceedings before any decisive action was taken, but soon after an answer appeared under the name of Samuel Mayart, a judge of the Court of Common Pleas in Ireland, who had been active in the parliamentary proceedings upon the *Declaration*. Manuscripts of the *Declaration* and Mayart's answer, in the possession of John Sterne, Bishop of Clogher, were printed in 1749 by Walter Harris as the second part of his *Hibernica*, after which they were placed in the library of Trinity College, Dublin, where they still remain.[2] The Trinity College manuscript of the *Declaration* contains the name of Richard Bolton, the Chancellor of Ireland, and its authorship is usually attributed to him, but Walter Harris, its editor, thinks it was written by Patrick Darcy, on the ground of its similarity to Darcy's *Argument* delivered in 1641.

Whoever its author may have been, the *Declaration* is a remarkable pamphlet. It is the most complete denial of the English Parliament's authority over Ireland based upon an exhaustive examination of the constitutional relations of the two countries since

---

[1] *Journals of the Irish House of Lords,* April 10 to April 18, 1644, printed in Harris, *Hibernica,* Part II, preface.

[2] The best accounts of these two books are in Monck Mason's *Parliaments in Ireland,* and Lord Chancellor Ball's *Legislative Systems in Ireland.*

Henry II's "conquest." Though written in 1644 or before, its fundamental argument is identical with that of Molyneux and Charles Lucas and Grattan, and the argument is supported by many of the precedents used a half century later in the much more famous book of Molyneux published in 1698, which appears on a comparison of the two to have been largely taken from the *Declaration,* though without acknowledgment. Grattan and Flood refer to Lucas and Swift and Molyneux, but few have mentioned Darcy or Bolton, the first to formulate the constitutional theory on which the Americans resisted the Declaratory Act of 1766, and the Irish opposed the similar act for Ireland of 1719, the theory on which the status of the Irish Parliament rested from 1782 to 1801, and on which in a sense it rests again since 1922. For Americans the *Declaration* is particularly important on account of the closeness of the parallel between its arguments and those of American statesmen from 1773 to 1776, particularly John and Samuel Adams. Charles Lucas's popularization of Darcy's doctrine occurred in 1748 in his *Addresses* to the free citizens of Dublin. It was the year of the appearance of Montesquieu's *De L'Esprit des Lois.* But how slight is the recognition of the work of Darcy or Bolton, of Molyneux and Lucas in the development of American constitutional institutions and political ideas, compared with the universal insistence of historians on the unquestioned influence of the erroneous deductions from the English constitution of the brilliant but often shallow Frenchman![1]

With the exception of Darcy's *Argument* of 1641, which is less complete, the *Declaration* is the first exposition of the American constitutional doctrine on parliamentary authority outside the realm. Nothing less than a reprint of it would be satisfactory, but I must be content with a summary only, and a very brief one.

The essential point of the constitutional contention of the *Declaration* is to "acknowledge superiority, allegiance, and subjection only to the King's sacred Majesty";[2] the assertion "that *Ireland* is a free and distinct kingdom of itself, the government whereof, is as political and regal, as the Kingdom of *England* is, and the King's Majesty, is supreme head of the body politick of *Ireland,* and that the Parliament of

---

[1] The actual connection between the Irish and American leaders is indicated by the fact that there is still extant "A Letter from the Town of Boston, to C. Lucas, Esq. . . . . Inclosing a Short Narrative of the Massacre Perpetrated there, in the Evening of the Fifth Day of March, 1770, by soldiers of the XXIXth Regiment, Quartered in the Town, . . . Printed by Order of the Town of Boston."

[2] *Hibernica,* Part II, p. 45.

England hath no more jurisdiction in *Ireland,* than ıt hath in *Scotland;*[1] in general, that "it cannot stand either in law or common reason, that one body politick should be subordinate or subject to the controul of the other."[2] This is a constitutional view of far-reaching significance, important not merely for Ireland but for all the King's dominions outside the realm. But it is obvious that the constitutional relations of England with Ireland before 1644, and of England with the other dominions as well, had been widely different from those between England and Scotland after 1603, and much closer. The main difference is that Ireland and the dominions had the English common law with an ultimate appeal to the courts of England, while Scotland had not. But according to the *Declaration* this in no way affects the English Parliament's *legislative* authority in any dominion; it remains no greater than in Scotland. For, "although writs of error to reverse judgments given in the King's-Bench in *Ireland* may be prosecuted in the King's-Bench in *England,* it doth not therefore follow, that the Parliament of *England* may repeal, alter, or change any laws or statutes of *Ireland,* or give new laws unto that kingdom: for if a writ of error be brought in *England*

[1] *Ibid.,* p. 41.
[2] *Ibid.,* p. 45.

to reverse a judgment given in the King's-Bench of *Ireland,* the Judges of *England* are not to alter or change the laws of *Ireland,* or to give judgment according to the laws in *England* in such case, but according to the laws in Ireland, where the first judgment was given." [a]

Notwithstanding this, the author was fully aware that many statutes passed before 1640 by the Parliament in England had been in force in Ireland, sometimes through express mention of Ireland, sometimes not. This difficulty he attempts to overcome by making a distinction between the English Parliament's judicial powers, in the affirmance or interpretation of the common law prevailing alike in both Kingdoms, and its legislative authority. The former the English Parliament had rightly exercised as the highest court of judicial appeal, and such acts in affirmation had been accepted and enforced in Ireland; but English acts "which were introductory or positive" had never been in force in Ireland before 1640 until they were re-enacted by the Irish Parliament. This famous distinction became the groundwork of the whole Irish constitutional claim to the very end and was reiterated by Molyneux, Lucas, Flood, Grattan, Monck Mason, and others. The bulk of the *Declaration* is devoted to

---

[a] *Hibernica,* Part II, p. 33.

an examination of the precedents from the time of
Henry II to that of the Long Parliament in an attempt
to prove this contention. Such, in briefest compass,
is the gist of Ireland's argument. Even this inadequate summary shows its great importance for the
Plantations as well. Mayart's answer, which is more
than four times as long as the *Declaration,* re-exam-
ines the precedents of Anglo-Irish constitutional relations and comes to a conclusion directly contradicting
the Irish claims in all points. His constitutional position will appear in the following extracts, which may
be profitably compared with the later views of Lord
Mansfield on the American question.

Ireland "was and is a member of England united
to it, and as a part and province of *England* governed." [1] "Ireland *is a part and member of* England,
*hath been governed by the Laws thereof, and subject
to the Laws made by the Parliament there."* [2]

"Many Cities and Corporations both in *England*
and *Ireland* have power to make by-laws to bind themselves . . . So *Ireland* had power to make laws to bind
themselves, and yet hath; . . . but hath not power to
make such laws as may bind or exclude the Parliament
of *England,* who hath power, and hath used to give

---

[1] *Hibernica,* Part II, p. 66.
[2] *Ibid.,* p. 160.

them laws, and to conform or revoke the laws which they shall make, as they please." [1]

The distinction made in the Declaration between affirmative and "introductory" laws Mayart refuses to accept as affecting Parliament's powers. "The power to make a declaratory law is one and the same with the power to make an introductory law, . . . and therefore if they have power to make one kind of law, they have power to make the other." [2] "For, to have power to declare what the law is, and to cause it to be executed, as it is declared, is the most sure and undeniable argument of power in them that command, and of subordination in them that obey, that can be." [3]

"Because the King's Bench in *England* hath power to repeal the judgments of law given in *Ireland,* and declare the law to be according to their judgments, contrary to the judgments given in *Ireland,* which they ought, and ever have obeyed, therefore, much more hath the Parliament of *England* power over *Ireland* to repeal or alter the laws, or give them new ones. And if they have any power over them, it must needs be in those things; because the power of Parliaments

---

[1] *Ibid.,* p. 174.

[2] *Ibid.,* p. 177.

[3] *Hibernica,* Part II, p. 179.

consists chiefly in altering, repealing, and giving new laws, and if this power be denied them, they shall have little or no power at all." [1]

To the argument of the *Declaration* that it is unjust that laws for Ireland should be made by Englishmen who are unacquainted with Irish conditions—an argument that sounds familiar enough to students of the American Revolution—it was Mayart's answer "that it is not now to be doubted, but they better know in *England* what Laws are in truth fit for them [the Irish], than they themselves do!" [2] Another of his arguments, not unlike the later claim of a "virtual representation," is the statement "that the liberties, lives, and estates, of those in *Ireland* should be bound by statutes made in *England,* because they are members of that Commonwealth, and parties to the Laws made there." [3] For it is evident, he says, "that Acts of Parliament of *England* did bind Dominions, as *Wales,* and County Palatines, as *Chester,* and that they were not such privies or parties as did send Knights or Burgesses thither. But as great a reason might have been alledged, that they ought to have been freed from being bound by the Parliament of *England,* as the Author

---

[1] *Ibid.,* pp. 182-183.
[2] *Ibid.,* p. 193.
[3] *Ibid.,* p. 195.

would have *Ireland* to be. And therefore I conclude, that it is necessary to every statute, that shall bind the Common Wealth, to have the Assent of the King, Lords, and Commons; so it is not necessary to have Knights and Burgesses from every Seignorie, Dominion, or County; but the assent of the three estates in Parliament there met together shall bind all the members of the Crown of *England,* and all others who are subject to their power." [1] "It is not the situation of the country, or because the sea runs between them, that makes a separation of the Government. . . . If the King of *England* should conquer any territories beyond sea, and give them the laws of *England,* and annex them to the Crown of *England,* I think none will say, that the distance of place will shake off the Power of the Government of *England;* no more will it do that of Ireland. . . . So it is in this case of *Ireland,* which being a member of the Crown of *England* is knit unto the same, and receives spirits (that is laws) from them: And therefore, if we consider *England* and *Ireland* as one body politic (which is not in all things to be compared to a natural body) and as *Ireland* is a member of the politic body of *England,* we may truly conclude from all that hath been

---

[1] *Hibernica,* Part II, pp. 196-197.

said, that *Ireland* is under the jurisdiction of the Parliament of *England* and subject thereunto." [1]

The period of the later sessions of the Long Parliament, of the Commonwealth and the Protectorate, was not productive of arguments of a constitutional kind on Anglo-Irish relations. Without a shadow of legal right, and with no distinction between affirming and "introductory" acts, Parliament imposed its absolute will alike upon the Realm and "the dominions and territories thereunto belonging," Ireland included.

The Restoration restored the King and for England the constitutional régime, but in the dominions it made no real change. And what the Restoration had retained, the Revolution established and made constitutional, so far as legal forms could do it. In their coronation oath the new sovereigns were "to govern the people of this Kingdom of Great Britain and the dominions thereunto belonging according to the Statutes in Parliament agreed on, and the respective laws and customs of the same." [2]

The oath as it stood from the accession of Edward II merely made this promise: *Concedis justas leges et consuetudines esse tenendas et promittis eas per te*

---

[1] *Ibid.*, pp. 224-225.

[2] L. G. Wickham Legg, *English Coronation Records,* Introduction, pp. xxxi, 326.

esse protegendas et ad honorem dei roborandas quas vulgus elegerit secundum vires tuas.   Respondebit Concede et promitto.[1]   At the coronation of Charles I the corresponding promise was, "Will you graunt to hold and keepe, the Lawes and rightfull Customes, which the Commonaltie of this your Kingdome have: and will you defend, and uphold them to the honor of *God,* so much as in you lyeth?"[2]   It was practically unchanged at the coronation of James II.[3]   Thus *quas vulgus elegerit,* "the Lawes and rightful customes which the Commonaltie of this your Kingdom have," comes to be, for the dominions, not what they "have," neither what they have "chosen" nor shall choose, nor what they themselves have "agreed on," but what a Parliament elected exclusively from the realm of England has "agreed on" for them.

Though the Revolution thus formally established the power of Parliament over the dominions, it was

---

[1] *Ibid.,* p. 88. For the interesting controversy between Prynne, who made *elegerit* refer to future action and thus practically gave the word the same meaning as the oath of 1689, and Dr. Brady who would have it refer only to *past* laws and customs, see Prynne, *The Soveraigne Power of Parliaments and Kingdomes* (1643), Part II, pp. 74-76; Robert Brady, *An Introduction to the Old English History* (1684), *The Glossary,* pp. 24-26, 36. See also, Stubbs, *Constitutional History of England,* ii, pp. 109, 331-332.

[2] Wickham Legg, *op. cit.,* p. 252.

[3] *Ibid.,* p. 297.

not long before this power was challenged again in Ireland. In 1698 appeared in Dublin a little book of 174 small pages with the title, *The Case of Ireland's Being Bound by Acts of Parliament in England Stated*, by William Molyneux of Dublin, Esq.

William Molyneux was a Protestant, member of the Irish Parliament, a mathematician of note, a close friend and correspondent of John Locke, whose political views he shared, and an ardent supporter of William III against the Jacobites; and his book itself was dedicated to William III.

This book is the more important as the work of a Williamite, who accepted to the fullest extent the existing connection of Ireland with the crown of England. But Molyneux rejects the authority of the English Parliament over Ireland as decisively as the Catholic Darcy half a century before, and the arguments of the *Declaration* are repeated and supported by many of the same precedents. Though the *Declaration* was not printed till half a century afterward, it seems most probable that one of the manuscripts of it had come into Molyneux's hands. But it would be unfair to imply that he was a mere copyist. Much of his material seems to be drawn from the *Declaration,* but it is put in new and more literary and systematic form, some new arguments of weight are added, and in addition the legislation of the English Parliament for Ireland from 1640 to 1698 is discussed. It was an epoch-making book, which deserved the sensation it created. From the time of its appearance until the present day, it is hardly too much to say, the constitutional problem with which it deals has been the most persistent and the most perplexing with which English statesmen have had to contend. Molyneux's thesis is Darcy's: before 1640 all English acts for Ireland became effective only when re-enacted in Ireland, except acts in affirmance of the Common Law. All other acts since are usurpations, unsupported by ancient precedent, and unconstitutional. Ireland is a separate Kingdom, independent of England and of its Parliament and subject only to the King.

On complaint against this book to the English Parliament, the Commons appointed a committee whose report was the basis for a unanimous resolution "that the said Book was of dangerous consequence to the crown and people of England, by denying the authority of the king and parliament of England, to bind the kingdom and people of Ireland, and the subordination and dependence that Ireland has, and ought to have upon England, as being united and annexed to the imperial crown of this realm." [1] This was followed

---

[1] *Parliamentary History*, v, 1181.

by an address to the King condemning the book and its doctrines, and requesting that all nceessary care be taken to restrain the Parliament of Ireland, to which the King replied, "That he would take care that what was complained of, might be prevented and redressed as the Commons desired." [1] Molyneux seems to have feared the consequences to himself, for he wrote to Locke a month before the Commons' action that he did "not think it adviseable for me to go on t'other side the Water" till he saw how Parliament would take the book. [2]

From this time on the question never slept long. The Parliaments of Anne and George I added materially to the already long list of "unconstitutional" acts binding Ireland, and the Irish agitation against them increased in volume and bitterness. In 1724 Swift wrote in *The Drapier's Letters,* "A 'dependent kingdom' is a modern term of Art, unknown, as I have heard, to all ancient civilians, and writers upon government. . . . I have looked over all the English and Irish statutes without finding any law that makes Ireland depend upon England, any more than England does upon Ireland. We have indeed obliged ourselves

---

[1] *Ibid.,* 1182.

[2] *Familiar Letters between Mr. John Locke and Several of his Friends,* 4th Edition, p. 213.

to have the same king with them, and consequently they are obliged to have the same king with us. For the law was made by our own Parliament, and our ancestors then were not such fools (whatever they were in the preceding reign) to bring themselves under I know not what dependence, which is now talked of without any ground of law, reason or common sense.

"Let whoever think otherwise, I, M. B. Drapier, desire to be excepted, for I declare, next under God, I *depend* only on the King my sovereign, and on the laws of my own country. . . . 'Tis true indeed, that within the memory of man, the Parliaments of England have sometimes assumed the power of binding this kingdom by laws enacted there, wherein they were at first openly opposed (as far as truth, reason and justice are capable of opposing) by the famous Mr. Molyneux, an English gentleman born here, as well as by several of the greatest patriots, and best Whigs in England; but the love and torrent of power prevailed. Indeed the arguments on both sides were invincible. For in reason, all government without the consent of the governed is the very definition of slavery: But in fact, eleven men well armed will certainly subdue one single man in his shirt." [1]

---

[1] *The Drapier's Letters,* edited by Temple Scott, Letter IV, pp. 113-115.

Swift's bitter sarcasm a little overshoots the mark. Molyneux was not answered merely by the "torrent of power." At least two reasoned replies were made immediately on the appearance of his book, *A Vindication of the Parliament of England, in answer to a book written by William Molyneux of Dublin, Esq., intituled 'The Case of Ireland's being bound by Acts of Parliament in England stated,'"* by John Cary, London, 1698; and *The History, and Reasons, of the Dependency of Ireland upon the Imperial Crown of the Kingdom of England. Rectifying Mr. Molyneux's State of the Case of Ireland's being bound by Acts of Parliament in England,* London, 1698. The second of these was by William Atwood, who might have some additional interest for Americans from the fact that he was later the King's Chief Justice in the Province of New York, where he had a rather stormy career on account of his rigid insistence upon the claims of the Courts of Admiralty, one of the great grievances of the Americans then and later in the constitutional struggle. Atwood was always an uncompromising champion of the widest stretch of Parliament's power, and in support of it he fell foul at one time or another of English Tories, Scots, Irish, and Americans.

But the "invincible argument" against Ireland to which Swift refers in the passage above was no doubt the *Declaratory Act* of 1719,[1] in which the English Parliament asserted its absolute power over Ireland in the precise terms used in 1766 to set forth the same authority over the American colonies. The constitutional issue was exactly the same in both cases, and the *Declaratory Act* of 1766, except for a few phrases, and the substitution of America for Ireland, is identical in tenor and wording with the *Declaratory Act* for Ireland in 1719, from which it was directly copied.[2]

---

[1] 6 Geo. I, chapter v.

[2] These two statutes are here placed in parallel columns for convenience of comparison:

Statute, Sixth George, I, Chapter Five (1719).	Statute, Sixth George III, Chapter Twelve (1766).
An Act for the better securing the Dependency of the Kingdom of *Ireland* upon the Crown of *Great Britain:*	An act for the better securing the Dependency of his Majesty's Dominions in *America* upon the Crown and Parliament of *Great Britain.*
I. Whereas the House of Lords of *Ireland* have of late, against Law, assumed to themselves a Power and Jurisdiction to examine, correct, and amend the Judgments and Decrees of the Courts of Justice in the Kingdom of *Ireland:*	Whereas several of the Houses of Representatives in his Majesty's Colonies and Plantations in America have of late, against Law, claimed to themselves, or to the General Assemblies of the same, the sole and exclusive Right of imposing Duties and Taxes upon his Majesty's Subjects in the said Colonies and Plantations; and have, in pursuance of such Claim, passed certain Votes, Resolutions, and Orders, derogatory to the Legislative Authority of Parliament, and inconsistent with the Dependency of the said Colonies and Plantations upon the Crown of *Great Britain:*
Therefore for the better securing of the Dependency of *Ireland* upon the Crown of *Great Britain,* May it please your most Excellent Majesty that it may be declared, and be it declared by the King's most Excellent Majesty, by and with the Advice and Consent of the Lords Spiritual and Temporal, and Commons, in this present Parliament assembled, and by the Authority of the same, That the said	May it therefore please your

The Irish agitation was renewed about the middle of the century in the widely read addresses and tracts

Kingdom of *Ireland* hath been, is, and of Right ought to be subordinate unto and dependent upon the Imperial Crown of *Great Britain*, as being inseparably united and annexed thereunto; and that the King's Majesty, by and with the Advice and Consent of the Lords Spiritual and Temporal, and Commons of *Great Britain* in Parliament assembled, h a d , hath, and of Right ought to have full Power and Authority to make Laws and Statutes of sufficient Force and Validity, to bind the Kingdom and People of *Ireland*.

II. And be it further declared and enacted by the Authority aforesaid, That the House of Lords of *Ireland* have not, nor of Right ought to have any Jurisdiction to judge of, affirm or reverse any Judgment, Sentence or Decree, given or made in any Court within the said Kingdom, and that all Proceedings before the said House of Lords upon any such Judgment, Sentence or Decree, are, and are hereby declared to be utterly null and void to all Intents and Purposes whatsoever.

most excellent Majesty, that it may be declared; and be it declared by the King's most excellent Majesty, by and with the Advice and Consent of the Lords Spiritual and Temporal, and Commons, in this present Parliament assembled, and by the Authority of the same, That the said Colonies and Plantations in *America* have been, are, and of Right ought to be, subordinate unto, and dependent upon, the Imperial Crown and Parliament of *Great Britain*: and that the King's Majesty, by and with the Advice and Consent of the Lords Spiritual and Temporal, and Commons of *Great Britain,* in Parliament assembled, had, hath, and of Right ought to have, full Power and Authority to make Laws and Statutes of sufficient Force and Validity to bind the Colonies and people of *America,* Subjects of the Crown of *Great Britain,* in all Cases whatsoever.

II. And be it further declared and enacted by the Authority aforesaid, That all Resolutions, Votes, Orders, and Proceedings, in any of the said Colonies or Plantations, whereby the Power and Authority of Parliament of *Great Britain,* to make Laws and Statutes as aforesaid, is denied or drawn into question, are, and are hereby declared to be, utterly null and void to all Intents and Purposes whatsoever.

of Charles Lucas, whose constitutional arguments are the same as Molyneux's,[1] but the man in his shirt was no match for the eleven in arms till the turn of the tide in the American war gave the first prospect of an actual attainment of the ideal sought by the Irish leaders for nearly one hundred and fifty years.

The brilliant leadership and oratory of Grattan and Flood in the Irish Parliament of 1780 renewed the old issue with all the old arguments and precedents, and this time pushed it to a triumphant practical conclusion in securing the repeal by the Parliament in England of the hated *Declaratory Act* of 1719; and later, though Grattan opposed it as unnecessary, a formal renunciation of any authority to bind the Parliament of Ireland in any case whatsoever. This was accompanied by the repeal of Poyning's Act by the Parliament of Ireland.[2]

Of these the Renunciatory Act is the most signifi-

---

[1] *Lucas's Addresses, Letters,* and other political writings were published separately at Dublin from time to time beginning in 1747. They were published in collective form in London in 1751, in two volumes, with the title, *"The Political Constitutions of Great Britain and Ireland Asserted and Vindicated."*

[2] See especially Grattan's speeches in support of his motion for a declaration of Irish rights of April 19, 1780, *Grattan's Speeches,* edited by his son, London, 1822, vol. i, p. 38ff., and on Feb. 22, 1782, *Ibid.,* p. 104ff.; and his speech on the repeal of the Irish Declaratory Act, of July 19, 1782, *Ibid.,* p. 145ff. The later of these speeches, together with others by Flood and

cant. It provides that "the said right claimed by the people of Ireland to be bound only by laws enacted by his Majesty and the Parliament of that Kingdom, in all cases whatever . . . shall be, and it is hereby declared to be, established and ascertained forever, and shall, at no time hereafter, be questioned or questionable." This was in 1783. Recently Mr. Sydney George Fisher wrote: "To suppose that there was *any part of the empire* to which the whole power of Parliament did not extend was as absurd in 1774 as it is today. It had the same authority over the people in America that it had over the people in London. . . . The colonists were, therefore, asking for independence of Parliament under an ancient form of the British Constitution—a form which had been abolished in the previous century by their friends the Whigs and William III."[1] I think I need add no comment.

---

others were also printed in *The Parliamentary Register or History of the Proceedings and Debates of the House of Commons of Ireland*, 2nd Edition, vol. i, Dublin, 1784. A fair and judicious account of these, and of the whole Irish constitutional question is given in Ball's *Legislative Systems in Ireland*. The English Statute repealing the Declaratory Act for Ireland was 22 George III, chapter 53. The Act renouncing Legislative authority over Ireland was 23 George III, chapter 28. See also, *The Irish Parliament from the Year* 1782 *to* 1800, by W. Ellis Hume Williams, Esq., London, 1879.

[1] *The True History of the American Revolution* (1902), pp. 132-133. *The Struggle for American Independence* (Philadelphia, 1908), vol. i, pp. 202-203.

The phraseology of the Renunciatory Act was adroitly framed with a purpose of avoiding, if possible, any commitment on the embarrassing question of the proper existence of "the right claimed by the people of Ireland" in the past, but, even disregarding the past, if it were a "right" at all, and if the plantations were alike in status with Ireland, as *Calvin's Case* and *Craw* v. *Ramsay* seem to indicate, one might hesitate to assert with too much confidence "that the colonists would have lost their case if the decision had turned upon an impartial consideration of the legal principles involved.[1] In the debates in the English House of Lords on the Renunciatory Act, Lord Abingdon declared that the Declaratory Act for Ireland of 1719 "was usurpation,"[2] and the Duke of Richmond went so far as to say "that no country had a right to legislate for another, either internally or externally, unless that other country choose to submit to such legislation."[3] In the same Parliament the Lords and Commons were debating on the final form of peace with their former American colonists.

The Irish constitutional parallel has now been fol-

---

[1] *Ante*, p. 17, Note 1.

[2] *Parliamentary History,* vol. 23, column 737.

[3] *Ibid.,* vol. 23, column 740. The whole of this debate, though rather listless, has an importance for this subject. See *Parliamentary History,* vol. 23, columns 16-48, 322-342, 730-757 *passim.*

lowed as far as it has any pertinence for the study of the American Revolution, but it must be evident that this Irish agitation, beginning in 1641 and carried on with few interruptions to the very end of the American constitutional struggle, furnishes material of the very greatest importance for the American historian. In both cases the ultimate issue was exactly the same, in both the circumstances were almost identical. Both Ireland and America conceded their connection with the English King, but both denied the authority of England's Parliament to bind them. The constitutional issue was raised in Ireland more than a century earlier than in America, merely because actual employment of Parliament's power over Ireland became a practical grievance there as soon as the power was assumed by the Long Parliament. In America, through more lax enforcement of law, greater distance and other causes, the issue was long delayed. But in both cases the claim to authority when made was exactly the same and made upon precisely the same grounds, and in both cases the opposition to this claim when it occurred was based fundamentally on the same conception of the relation existing between the realm of England and the other dominions of the King.

The fact that the Irish insistence upon these common constitutional claims runs so much further back than the American ought in itself to constitute an argument for their thorough study among the causes of the American Revolution. Of all constitutional parallels to the American Revolution, this Irish one is the closest, the most definite and conscious, and the longest in continuance that can be found in British history. It begins a century and a quarter before the same issue was seriously agitated in America, it continued side by side with the American struggle till its very close, and it proceeded at every point upon a carefully considered interpretation of the British constitution and its historical precedents. The parallel is so striking that the wonder grows that it has to such an extent been ignored by the writers on the constitutional history of America in the period of the Revolution.

The subsequent failure of the Irish experiment in no way affects either the importance of the constitutional struggle before 1782 or the merits of the Irish claims made in that period. From the constitutional point of view that failure was mainly due to the fact that legislative independence is unworkable without self-government, under any régime of "responsible government." "Dominion status," as it is now called, differs from the position of Ireland between 1782 and 1801 simply in this, that "dominion status" implies self-government in fact without legislative independence in law, while Ireland then had the legislative independence without any self-government. Since 1922 southern Ireland has more than any other dominion in having both self-government and legislative independence guaranteed by law, and this gives a promise for the new Irish Free State which Grattan's Ireland never could have had. It required the utter collapse of the old colonial system in the thirteen North American colonies, an impending collapse of the same system in the remaining continental colonies half a century later, the repeated assaults of men like Buller and Wakefield and Lord Durham upon a succession of stubborn and doctrinaire Colonial Secretaries and still more stubborn under Secretaries, before the light finally broke in and any hopeful solution of the perplexing problem of dominion rule could be found. Parliamentary government is probably the most developed form of representative institutions now known; in advance even of the "presidential" form evolved here in America, but it has this defect of its merits, that it makes "the government of dependencies" illogical and almost impossible. For its very perfection in the mother country exaggerates the dependent status of the "British possessions." Lord John Russell and Sir George Cornewall Lewis in their insistence upon the mutual contradiction of "self-government" and "dependency" were logically right, and Sir Robert Borden's phrase of 1917 for the British Empire amply proves them so—"Autonomous Nations of an Imperial Commonwealth."

Theirs was much the same argument in a different application as Lord Mansfield's assertion in 1766 against America, that "in every government the legislative power must be lodged somewhere, and the executive must likewise be lodged somewhere. In Great Britain the legislative is in Parliament, the executive in the crown."[1] To all these precisians the warning of the late Professor Maitland is equally applicable: "Some friendly critics would say that in the past we could afford to accept speciously logical but brittle theories because we knew that they would never be subjected to serious strains. Some would warn us that in the future the less we say about a supralegal, suprajural plenitude of power concentrated in a single point at Westminster—concentrated in one single organ of an increasingly complex commonwealth— the better for that commonwealth may be the days that are coming."[2] The history of Ireland and America

---

[1] *Parliamentary History*, vol. xvi, column 173.

[2] Gierke, *Political Theories of the Middle Age*, Introduction, p. xliii.

discloses a few strains even in the past that all but broke in pieces some of these "brittle theories." But, though logically right, these men were practically wrong and lamentably blind—to say nothing of law— in opposing the only hopeful practical solution for a problem that had existed since 1640 and had already almost wrecked the Empire. Dependence had to be lessened and self-government correspondingly in- creased. The inevitable outcome was a league of autonomous nations, but it is a league at least, and such the present British Empire really is in fact, if not in law, so far as the "self-governing colonies" are con- cerned. Such a problem as this could never have arisen but for parliamentary government. It was the genius of Wakefield and his associates to see that par- liamentary government also presented the only solu- tion, that the essential principle of the new limited monarchy that left wide powers in the Crown which none but the representatives of the people could exercise, might now save the Empire as it had already saved the realm. That solution began in 1847 but its application to Ireland was delayed till 1922.

I have said that the problem as well as the solution was created by the institution of "parliamentary gov- ernment," and that that problem was made more diffi-

cult with every further development of cabinet government till the final solution was found.   Mere legislative independence might probably have solved the
Irish question in the seventeenth century, because the
Irish executive was still really the King's deputy in
fact as well as in law, and was little subject to the
King's other parliament in England.   But two centuries later it had become impossible, for with each
advance of "responsible government" in England, all
the servants of the Crown became in greater degree
subject to the commands of the English Parliament
and the English Parliament alone.   In corresponding
degree the people of Ireland and the dominions became more and more subject to the control of the
people of England.   As England's "self-government"
increased, the "dependency" of the dominions increased
also, a dependency now of one dominion on another,
a subordination of one people to another.   Just in pro-
portion as responsible government advanced in England mere legislative independence therefore became
more unsatisfactory as a solution of the problem of any
dominion.   But these aspects have mainly to do with
the period in the Empire and Ireland, especially between 1782 and 1922; they affect in no important way
the older problem of the status of Ireland in its strictly
legal or constitutional aspect, or of the old colonial

ject allows; he might as well accept probable reasoning from a mathematician as require demonstrative proofs from a rhetorician."[1]   Legal precedents have at all times been cited as conclusive proof of facts as existing at the time of their citation, but they do not always constitute such "demonstrative proofs."   In this case of affirmative acts, it is confidently asserted by the Irish that certain old acts of the English Parliament were in their nature merely in affirmance of the common law already existing, and it is denied just as confidently by their English opponents.   The difficulty lies in the fact that the distinction itself between acts declaratory of the old law and acts introductive of new, is a distinction which was not clearly present in the minds of the Parliaments by which many of these old laws were enacted.   The distinction is a comparatively late one, employed by the courts long afterward in the interpretation of statutes, but not contemplated at all when many of the statutes in question were first formulated.   Another cause of uncertainty is the undeveloped form of Parliament at the time of the earliest enactments in question, as well as the vagueness of our knowledge of the King's relation to it.   But possibly the greatest indefinite-

---

[1] *Eth. Nic.,* I, 1.

ness of all is due to the fact that it is well-nigh impossible now to know what actually constituted a "statute" at a time when the very term itself had not yet grown into its modern definite technical meaning. To establish conclusively in such circumstances that a given "statute" was or was not in affirmance is a task more difficult than the controversialists on either side would have admitted, and we may sometimes have to content ourselves with a mere probability in cases where they demanded and believed they had established a demonstrative proof. It is hard indeed to revive with clearness ideas and conceptions or forms of procedure on which contemporaries themselves were neither clear nor definite. No single fault has been the source of so much bad history as the reading back of later and sharper distinctions into earlier periods where they have no place. If we really want truth, we may be compelled to be satisfied with somewhat less than absolute demonstration. It would be better to be content with "a definitely conceived indefiniteness," as Maitland so happily puts it.

For enactments of the period *after* the distinction between affirmative and introductory statutes had become clearly recognized, statements may be made with more confidence perhaps, but even there our difficulty is by no means at an end, for new law and affirmations

are not labelled as such and can only be distinguished
by a careful comparison of the content of the acts
themselves with the law in existence when the enactments were made. Thus Molyneux says of the *Statutum Hiberniae,* 14 Henry III, " . . . 'tis manifest,
that this *Statutum Hiberniae* was no more than a Cer-
tificate of what the *common Law of England* was in
that Case, which *Ireland* by the *Original Compact* was
to be governed by, And shews no more, that therefore
the Parliament of *England* may bind *Ireland,* than it
would have proved, that the Common Wealth of *Rome*
was subject to *Greece,* if, after *Rome* had received the
Law of the *Twelve Tables,* they had sent to *Greece* to
know that the Law was, in some Special Case." [1]

In this particular case the words of the act itself
seem to justify Molyneux's interpretation, but others
are by no means so clear, and Atwood thinks he has
cited several clearly "introductory" ones. [2]

The "proofs" adduced by Molyneux and his opponents must obviously be sought in their own books: no
brief summary would be fair to them, and in a short
essay like this space could be found for no more. I
must be content with an indication of my own im-
pressions derived from these books and from some

---

[1] *The Case Stated,* pp. 87-88.
[2] *The History, and Reasons,* p. 114ff.

study of the institutions of the period from which their precedents are taken.

Any decision on the relative merits of the assertions of Molyneux and his opponents depends so much on the true nature of the institutions and of men's ideas about them at the time of the disputed statutes, that something must be briefly set forth concerning these. I am, therefore, taking the liberty of quoting on this subject from a paper contributed by me some years ago to a volume of studies in commemoration of the seven hundredth anniversary of Magna Carta, and entitled *Magna Carta and Common Law:* [1]

"*First.*—Enactments of substantive law in England in the later Middle Ages were made for the general purpose of affirming the law already approved or of removing abuses which hindered its due execution— 'pur surement garder les Loies ove due execution et hastif remedie pur abusion de la Loye an usurpation." [2]

"Such affirmance implied frequent interpretation, the supplying of additional penalties to secure proper execution, and even supplemental enactments for the same purpose. This eventually led to changes in the

---

[1] *Magna Carta Commemoration Essays,* edited for the Royal Historical Society by Henry Elliot Malden, 1917, pp. 122-179.

[2] "Pronunciato" of the Parliament of 13 Henry IV (1411), "Rot. Parl." iii. 647.

law itself, but such changes came gradually and in the
main only incidentally, and were not the main purpose of enactment. Repeal of the laws used and
approved is in the beginning not thought of. It
comes very gradually, and in the guise of the removal
of provisions which have wrongfully interpreted or
added to the old law and tended to the introduction of
abuses rather than the removal of them. The sub-
stance of the old law itself is in theory not repealable,
at least in early times. When statutes are repealed the
oft-repeated reason is that they are against the law
of the land or prerogative. Repeal is strictly in the
beginning, nothing more than a remedy 'pur abusion
de la Loye en usurpation.' Occasionally, in times of
disorder, whole Parliaments were repealed in the fourteenth and fifteenth centuries, but the reason alleged
is usually that their summons is irregular or their acts
unlawful. It is only at a comparatively late period
that the repeal of statutes is openly avowed as one of
the purposes of Parliament; even then such a power
is hardly considered as reaching the central principles
of the common law. On the contrary, an examination
of parliamentary rolls of the fourteenth and fifteenth
centuries will show that the first business of a Parliament is the re-enactment or affirmance of the whole
body of the fundamental law, including the statutes of

the King's predecessors. This is nearly always stated among the purposes of the Parliament in the 'Pronunciationes,' and it is almost invariably prayed for first among the petitions of the Commons. It would not be beyond the truth to say that in this period, Parliament was, in its 'legislative' capacity, above anything else, an affirming body, for such affirmations *en bloc* are almost invariable.[1] It is only in the latter part of this period that the Commons in their petition for the affirmance of preceding enactments begin to add the significant phrase, 'et nient repellez.'[2] There is a remarkable, and possibly not accidental, similarity between these repeated affirmations at the opening of each Parliament and the earlier proclamations of the King's peace, at the beginning of each reign.

"*Second*.—Participation in the enactment of such laws is based on the theory that the binding enactment of a law can be made only by those whom it touches. It must be a law 'approbata utentium,' to use Bracton's phrase. If an enactment is to bind the clergy, the clergy must assent; to one binding the baronage, the barons must assent; a provision affecting merchants

---

[1] See "Rot. Parl." iv. cxxx, No. 10.

[2] For repeal, see "Rot. Parl." iii. 352 A; *ibid.*, pp. 425 A-B; 426 A, 442 A; stat. i. Hen. IV, cap. iii.; stat. ii. Hen. IV, cap. xiii.; "Rot. Parl." v. 374 A-B; stat. 39 Hen. VI, cap. i.; "Rot. Parl." vi. 191 A. See also "4 Inst," p. 52.

only is binding on account of their consent alone; and
the law of particular districts is recognised as valid
'more approbata utentium.' But likewise, 'what
touches *all* should be approved by *all*.'[1] And what
touches all is the law common to all—the 'lex communis, lex terrae, lex regni.'

"On this basis of consent Glanvil had tried to fit
feudal conditions into Roman terms, by saying that
the people had enacted a law that had been 'approved'
by immemorial custom; much in the same way that
Roman lawyers, ages before him, had interpreted the
'uti legassit' of the Twelve Tables in the development
of the law of testamentary succession. If this were
true, it would not be absurd to assimilate English custom with Roman 'lex.' It certainly was observed 'pro

---

[1] This famous sentence appeared in the writs of summons to
the clergy for the model Parliament of 1295 ("Parl. Writs," vol.
i., p. 30). The writs begin as follows: "Sicut lex justissima,
provida circumspectione sacrorum principum stabilita, hortatur
et statuit ut quod omnes tangit ab omnibus approbetur, sic et
nimis evidenter ut communibus periculis per remedia provisa
communiter obvietur." The "lex" here referred to is probably
from Justinian's "Code," 5, 59, 5, where nothing of a political
character is referred to, but only the common action of several
"co-tutores" appointed under a will or otherwise. The original
words are, "ut, quod omnes similiter tangit, ab omnibus com-
probetur." It is interesting to note that in the supplementary
title "De Regula Juris" at the end of the "Sext," published three
years after Edward's writs, in 1298, Boniface the Eighth includes this maxim as regula xxix., "Quod omnes tangit, debet
ab omnibus approbari."

lege.' All this is clear enough for local and particular customs. But what of the common law? How can it really be said to be enacted, affirmed, and 'approbata utentium omnium'?

"For much of the thirteenth century the baronage, lay and ecclesiastical, made good their claim that they alone were the 'populus'; that 'all' included none beyond themselves. 'Populus' is frequently used in that sense at that time, and their assent seems to have been considered the assent of the realm. But by the fourteenth century this was changed. Other communes besides theirs were making themselves felt in the national councils, the 'communitas bacheleriæ Angliæ,'[1] and the communities of the towns, who considered themselves a part of the 'communitas Angliæ'[2] to which the 'lex communis' applied. It is a striking fact that Edward's principle that what touches all should be approved by all was carried no further than those communities until the Reform Bills of the nineteenth century. Those had a right to participate in the enactment of common law, to whom common law applied, and by the fourteenth century the communes of the counties and the towns were able successfully to vindi-

---

[1] "Annals of Burton," p. 471, quoted in Stubbs. "Select Charters" (ninth edition), p. 331.
[2] *Ibid.*

cate in Parliament their claim to be a part of the 'po-pulus' to which that law and all provisions affirming it were common.

"It is clear that such a principle could not be en-forced, and could indeed hardly arise, before the com-position of Parliament was settled on the basis which it retained until the legislation of the nineteenth cen-tury. Naturally, while that composition was still un-settled, this principle was doubtful. Even if a law must be 'utentium approbata,' how could the whole 'communitas Angliæ' consent in Parliament? At first, apparently, while the composition of Parliament fluc-tuated, there was doubt as to the validity of an enact-ment until it had been proclaimed locally throughout the realm. Only gradually did the theory arise that the whole of England was constructively in Parliament; that they were all assumed to be there consenting to what Parliament did. The theory of representation was complete in the fourteenth century. The fact that much of the representation was only 'virtual' need give us little concern, when we remember that this remained equally true for five hundred years after, and that to a certain extent it is true today. This theory then did not necessarily give to the estates in Parliament alone the right to legislate for particular persons, classes, or places. That might be done by the King by charter or

otherwise with the assent of those only who were affected.   Neither did it require the assent of 'all' the
estates in Parliament unless that assent was given to
some enactment which touched them all.   The one
thing that obviously did touch them all was an enactment affecting the 'lex communis.'   To that the assent
of 'all' was necessary." [1]

If the statements made above are correct, one may
say that in the period before the clear distinction arose
between such acts as only affirmed existing law, and
such acts as introduced new, "statutes" were in reality
practically all in affirmance; that when "statute" finally
came to mean a definite kind of enactment at all, it
meant at first nothing but an enactment or affirmance
of customary law that existed before it.   For this period, then—the period before the distinction above appears—the probabilities seem to favor the interpretation of Molyneux and his predecessors rather than that
of his English opponents.

For any consideration of the period following this,
the period when a distinction between affirming and

---

[1] *Magna Carta Commemoration Essays,* pp. 140-145.   It is only
fair to say that my interpretation has not been unopposed.   See
the able arguments *contra* of Mr. T. F. T. Plucknett, *Statutes
and their Interpretation in the First Half of the Fourteenth
Century,* Cambridge, 1922 (*Cambridge Studies in English Legal
History*).   After careful consideration of these objections, I still
adhere to the fundamental position set forth in 1917.

"introductive" laws is clearly apprehended, we must first discover if possible when they were first so apprehended.

And with one statement of Mr. Plucknett in supposed criticism of my theory of affirmance mentioned above, I find myself in entire agreement; "there is no trace in the Year Books of the first three Edwards of anyone thinking that statutes were essentially affirmations of common law. . . . Nothing resembling a theory of law and legislation is to be found. Fourteenth century England was content to see the fact and leave the theory alone."[1] My original contention merely was that affirmance was a fact not a theory. The theory could naturally hardly be put back beyond the period when legislation had begun to be conscious. Two things are not usually contrasted before they are both clearly apprehended. Confirmation as a theory of enactment was not likely to appear before "legislation" made it obvious, and conscious "legislation" is rather hard to find much before the fifteenth century. The *theory* of affirmance is no earlier. I cannot be sure of its existence before the middle of the fifteenth century or even then. Fitzherbert's *Abridgement,* published early in Henry VIII's reign says nothing of affirmance. In Brooke's *Abridgement,* probably written

---

[1] *Statutes and their Interpretation,* pp. 30-31.

in the reign of Mary, the distinction is clear.[1] The conscious distinction between acts declaratory of new law and acts in affirmance of old is one, then, that can be applied with entire safety for our purpose practically only to Tudor and post-Tudor enactments for Ireland.

Certain of these without a doubt make new law, which is sometimes tacitly, sometimes expressly extended to Ireland. Molyneux admits this, but declares that before 1640, at least, these were always re-enacted by the Parliament in Ireland before they were enforced there, that those not thus re-enacted were never in force, and therefore that the only English Statutes enforced without re-enactment were those in affirmance of the common law. The issue here is clear-cut enough. In proof Molyneux is able to cite a number of English acts which certainly were re-enacted in Ireland, and the absence of further record of re-enactments he accounts for by the undoubted fact of the destruction or loss of many Irish records. He points to the wholesale enactment of all earlier English statutes by the

---

[1] The references in Brooke are to be found in *Parlement,* Nos. 29, 70, 84, 90, 101, and 108. His earliest reference is to a case in *Y. B.* 36 H. vi, No. 3; others are 18 E. iv, No. 16; and 21 H. vii, No. 21. (In the Edition of 1679 it should be No. 20.) A reading of these cases does not make it clear that the *theory* of affirmance is definitely expressed in them.

Irish Parliament at Drogheda in the tenth year of
Henry VII (Poyning's Act),[1] and asserts of English
acts introductive of new law that since that time "it
was never made a Question whether they should Bind
Ireland, without being Allow'd in Parliament here; till
of very late years this Doubt began to be moved."[2]
Poyning's Act itself he regards as a proof of his contention, an Irish act designed to prevent Irish legislation hostile to England. "But this was a needless
Caution, if the King, and Parliament of *England,* had
Power at any time to revoke or annul any such Proceedings."[3]

---

[1] *The Case Stated,* p. 69.

[2] *Ibid.,* p. 71.

[3] *Ibid.,* pp. 160-161. An act on the Irish statute roll of 38
Henry VI (1460) seems to come nearest to an official statement
on this matter. In that year it was enacted "at the request of
the Commons," "That whereas the land of Ireland is and at
all times has been corporate of itself, by the ancient laws and
customs used in the same, freed of the burden of any special
law (*especiale ley*) of the realm of England, save only such laws
as by the lords spiritual and temporal and the commons of the
said land had been in Great Council or Parliament there held,
admitted, accepted, affirmed and proclaimed, according to sundry
ancient statutes thereof made (*auoient eu en graund Counseile
ou parliament illeosques tenuz admisez acceptez affermez & pro-
clamez acordaunt as plusours auncientz estatutes dent faitz*),"
etc. . . . *Statute Rolls of the Parliament of Ireland,* edited by
Henry F. Berry (Dublin, 1910), vol. ii, pp. 644-645. These
participles are rather significant, and "made" is not among them.
Another important instance was in 13 Edward II (1320) at a
Parliament in Dublin, where it was agreed "that the Statutes of

Needless to say, this is all interpreted differently by Cary and Atwood, and a decision is difficult. Re-enactment in Ireland in itself is no absolute proof of the English Parliament's inability to bind Ireland. In fact, neither absolute proof nor disproof can be found, as no declaration of Parliament's claim exists, nor any direct repudiation of such a claim in Ireland.

Though this distinction between acts of affirmation and those introductory of new law was a question of greater direct importance for Ireland than for America, the conclusions as to Parliament's authority based on this distinction are equally important for both, and the Irish history of this distinction becomes properly a part of American constitutional history.

It would be a mistake, however, to assume that the

Westminster the First and the Second, of Merton, of Marlborough and Gloucester be held, and the other statutes made in England by the King and his council be read and examined before the King's council between this and the next parliament, and there published, *and that the points which are applicable to the people and the peace of the land of Ireland be from thenceforth confirmed and held,* saving always the good customs and usages of the land." Berry, *op. cit.,* I, pp. 281-283. The italics are not in the original. The claim is here practically made that English law is in force in Ireland on account of a "reception." For a similar claim in America as to early English statutes, see Maryland's Constitution of 1776, section III of the Declaration of Rights, Thorpe, *Constitutions,* III, 1687.

Another instance referred to by Darcy in his argument occurred in 1410 (XI Henry IV), Berry, *op. cit.* I, p. 520.

distinction itself played no direct part outside the
United Kingdom. In 1720, Richard West, then counsel to the Board of Trade and later Lord Chancellor
of Ireland, advised the Board that "all statutes in affirmance of the common law" passed in England before a colony's settlement were in force in the colony,
but "no statutes" made since unless the colonies are
particularly mentioned.[1] It is interesting to note that
this opinion, given the year after the *Declaratory Act*
for Ireland, makes no direct claim for acts not in affirmance passed either before or after settlement,
though this claim is distinctly made in later opinions
of this kind.[2]

In Ireland itself this issue was not sharply raised
until 1641 and the Irish repudiation was then prompt
and decisive. Standing by themselves, the Irish precedents from 1485 to 1641 hardly warrant a safe judgment either way, but fortunately they do not quite
stand by themselves. There exists some evidence in

---

[1] Forsyth, *Cases and Opinions on Constitutional Law,* p. 1;
Chalmers, *Colonial Opinions* (American Edition, 1858), p. 206.

[2] Joint opinion of Attorney General DeGrey and Solicitor General Willes, in 1767. Forsyth, *op. cit.,* p. 3; Chalmers, *op. cit.,* p.
211. For other opinions on this point, see Forsyth, *op. cit.,* chap. i,
with the editor's note; Chalmers, *op. cit.,* pp. 206-232, and St. G.
L. Sioussat, *The Theory of the Extension of English Statutes to
the Plantations,* reprinted in *Select Essays in Anglo-American
Legal History* (Cambridge, 1907), vol. i, p. 416.

other dominions of the King and in the general nature
of the fealty to the King as defined in *Calvin's Case,*
which, taken in connection with these Irish precedents,
tends, in my opinion, to incline the balance of probability decidedly towards the Irish view of Parliament's
powers.   To these I must now turn, and first to such
as are furnished by the relations between Parliament
and other early dominions outside Ireland.

One of the most interesting features of the British
Empire to a student of the growth of institutions is
its lack of constitutional uniformity.   Hardly any two
of the dominions which constitute it began at the same
time or in the same way.   For this reason it is impossible usually to find an exact parallel or precedent for
the institutions of one in another of the British colonies or possessions.   But some have much closer re-
semblances than others, and on the basis of the relation between the realm of England and the dominions.
Ireland as it was before the American Revolution had
probably more constitutional points in common with
the American colonies than any other dominion of the
Empire.   There were differences, of course.   Ireland
was a separate kingdom, and the colonies were not, but
it is hard to see any important constitutional results of
this, either legal or practical.   Ireland's connection with
England, also, was alleged, though denied as well, to

be the result of a conquest, while most of the American colonies originated in settlement. These are about the only differences of any importance at all, and their constitutional significance is not great. Admitting the actual "conquest" of Ireland, which Molyneux denied, it is not easy to see, as Molyneux also pointed out, why permanent subordination should necessarily follow. Besides, both Ireland and the Plantations were theo- retically at least sharers in the common law of England. If Ireland was conquered, there were parts of North America, such as New York, not entirely unlike it, and if most of the thirteen colonies were "plantations," formed by settlement, it was also true that the first English "plantations," and the first English settlements called a colony were in Ulster.[1] In most constitutional aspects, Ireland and America were alike, and the his- tory of early Anglo-Irish constitutional relations is properly a part of American constitutional history, for rightly or wrongly Ireland and America were com- monly linked together, as "Dominions of the Crown,"

---

[1] The original meaning of "plantation" had reference not to the lands occupied by new settlers as is usually assumed, but to the removal or transplanting of the settlers themselves, the other meaning is a secondary one. Hobbes uses the expression "a plan- tation of men," and it is not uncommon in the sixteenth and seventeenth centuries. Edmund Spenser and Sir John Davis habitually refer to the Ulster settlements as "colonies" and "plan- tations."

with a common status, different from "Dominions of
the King." If such a distinction as this is to be rejected for America, as John Adams insisted it must,
then evidence of value on the general question should
be found in Ireland, and in fact it is found. Ireland,
therefore, as the closest parallel to the thirteen colonies
in the whole of the old colonial Empire, has furnished
the greater part of the evidence that I have had to
employ in attempting to clarify the American issues.

But, notwithstanding some differences, there are
other parts of the Empire that tend to corroborate the
evidence of Ireland. Scotland has a very different history in this respect, but one might say that the status
which Scotland undeniably had as a mere "dominion
of the King" and not "of the Crown" was the same
as that demanded as of right for Ireland by the Irish
and for America by the Congress in 1774. This demand could only be justified by proving that there
really was no essential difference between the relations of England with Ireland or America and those
between England and Scotland. If Ireland was the
closest constitutional parallel to colonial America,
Scotland was its constitutional ideal; and if there was
no sound constitutional justification for the distinction
between "dominions of the King" and "dominions of
the Crown," we must think America's attempt to real-

ise this ideal not entirely unjustifiable. Scotland has thus an interest for the historian of the American Revolution, but the Anglo-Scottish relations hardly need a review here.[1]

The parallels of Wales, Chester, Durham, Berwick, and the Marches in general are not sufficiently close to furnish evidence of much value on either side of the issue with which I am here concerned. Whatever the status of any of these may have been at any time, the relations of all were affected by their actual physical contact with the realm which as we can now see inevitably marked them out for complete ultimate absorption in it. The chief importance of their relations for the American issue is the evidence they furnish on the question of taxation. For the American argument

---

[1] As early as 1305 there is some evidence that Edward I had in mind at least a "legislative union" between England and Scotland, *The Acts of the Parliament of Scotland,* vol. i, p. 13 (Record Commission) ; but the Scots themselves upset all such plans for three hundred years. The *Instrument of Government* of 1653 provided for representation of both Scotland and Ireland and representatives for both sat in Parliaments of the Protectorate. See Gardiner, *Constitutional Documents of the Puritan Revolution,* p. 317; C. S. Terry, *The Cromwellian Union (Scottish History Society),* 1902; *Burton's Diary,* vol. iv, pp. 94, 99, 100, 101, 210, 211, 213, 217, 219. For the reference to these interesting passages from *Burton's Diary,* relating to the question of the right of Scottish and Irish members to sit in the Parliament of the Protectorate, I am indebted to Mr. Marcus L. Hansen, who was kind enough to put at my disposal the results of his researches.

based upon the constitution of the Empire they are less important than those dominions, which like America, are physically separate from Great Britain and hence not naturally destined to complete assimilation. Scotland would probably have been in the same position as Chester in this respect, but for Bannockburn.

Temporary earlier English possessions like Tournay or Calais may also have some importance for the taxation issue, but they have little bearing on the imperial question.

But within the British Empire, though not within the "United Kingdom," and separated from England by the sea, are two European "British Possessions," one of which is today the most ancient surviving dominion of the King of England outside the realm itself. The two are the Isle of Man and the Channel Islands, and in the latter may be found by far the oldest, and with the exception of Ireland, and in some respects possibly Scotland, the closest parallel to the status of colonial America in the eighteenth century, a parallel and a precedent which, on account of its age, has more bearing on the American issue than any other save that of Ireland itself; and like Ireland, it deserves more attention than it has received. Like most of the thirteen English colonies in North America in the eight-

eenth century the Channel Islands had not been conquered, like all the colonies they had their own legislative assemblies. Unlike the thirteen colonies and
Ireland, but like Canada and Scotland, they had neither
received nor inherited the common law of England.
They were not taxed by the English Parliament, and
they never have been to this day. They make no con-
tribution to the British army or navy. Should we
have called them a "Dominion of the King" or a "Dominion of the Crown" in 1774, if we accepted such a
distinction as a valid one? There seems little doubt
as to which status they would have claimed for themselves. The act in regard to smuggling passed by the
British Parliament in the midst of the conflict with
Napoleon was particularly objected to by these islanders, and as late as 1805 pamphlets were published by
magistrates of Guernsey to prove that such an act
could have no binding force in the islands. England
had never conquered the islands, but rather their Duke
—for they had been a part of Normandy—had really
conquered England. They had never therefore been a
fief of the King of England at all, but only of the
Norman Duke, who had later made himself lord of
England as well as Normandy. They were in no other
wise connected with England at all. The lord of Eng-

land who in the realm had also become *Rex,* in Guernsey remained only *Dux.* Such reasoning would play havoc with the authority of a parliament of the realm over Guernsey, and it would even destroy the argument for the authority of an English privy council as well, but can it be said that it is wholly without historical justification? The practical conclusion drawn by these writers was that the English Parliament could pass no act affecting the ancient rights or privileges of the islands, but could only *recommend* such a measure to the King and Council who might then transmit it to the islands or not as they pleased. But even should they determine to transmit an act of this kind, these writers asserted that the bailiff and jurats in the islands were not bound to register it, were in fact forbidden by their own law and their oaths of office to do so if it were against the constitution of Guernsey, and that without this registration by the local magistrates the act had in Guernsey no binding force whatever.[1]

In the debates on the Smuggling Prevention Bill[2] in Parliament itself, counsel for petitioners against the bill from the Channel Islands reiterated the historical claims of the islands in the strongest terms, even as-

---

[1] William Berry, *The History of the Island of Guernsey,* pp. 223-224.

[2] 45 George III, chap. cxxi.

serting that the islands once "had as good, if not a better right, originally to legislate for Great Britain then, than Great Britain had to legislate for them," [1] an argument that seemed to impress certain members of the House,[2] of whom one expressed the interesting opinion that it was a strange argument "that the independence of those islands was less injured by being governed under the more arbitrary principle of edicts from the King in Council, than under the constitutional protection of a British Parliament." [3] Mr. Windham said that from the argument of counsel "it certainly was a doubtful question, whether this country had a right to legislate for Guernsey and Jersey, or not," and he proposed an investigation of the whole matter.[4] In the end the bill was passed, but with an amendment inserted by the Chancellor of the Exchequer to satisfy the constitutional claims of the islanders,[5] which provided that the trial of all cases of alleged breach of the act committed in the Channel Islands should be "inquired of, examined, tried, and determined in the said islands," while all such offences "committed else-

---

[1] *Hansard's Parliamentary Debates,* 1st Series, vol. v, p. 629, (1805).

[2] *Ibid.,* 630.

[3] *Ibid.,* 632.

[4] *Ibid.,* 647.

[5] *Hansard's Parliamentary Debates,* 1st Series, vol. v, p. 646.

where out of the United Kingdom" might be tried in "any county of the United Kingdom." [1]

The precedents cited for these conflicting views run back as far as the reign of John and even further, and as usual they are not always entirely convincing either way, particularly the earliest of them. But it may be at least doubted whether the general claim of the islanders, so strong *prima facie* on account of the admitted facts of mediæval history, has not put a burden of proof upon the imperialists which all the evidence they have been able to submit has not conclusively overthrown. It is, to say the least, neither an impossible nor an unwarrantable conclusion from these precedents as a whole, that the exercise of parliamentary authority over these islands before the period of the Interregnum is not definitely and conclusively established, and that the exercise of such an authority afterward may therefore not unreasonably be regarded as without sufficient historical justification and hence "unconstitutional" and "illegal." This is precisely the contention which the Irish in 1641 began to make for Ireland, and the Americans for America in 1774. It is impossible here adequately to recount these precedents, and the use made of them, and I must be content with a mere reference to the places where they may be

---

[1] Statute 45 George III, chap. cxxi, section xii (1805).

found;[1] but I cannot refrain from noticing briefly a few official statements of the Judicial Committee of the Privy Council, and the opinions of one or two English constitutional authorites upon these important questions, some of them in very recent years.

Possibly the most important earlier case was one before the Judicial Committee of the Privy Council in 1853.[2] Three orders in council had been passed and sent to Jersey for registration for removal of some of the antiquated features of the legal procedure of that island. This was regarded by the States of Jersey (the local legislative assembly), as a violation of their ancient rights, and they petitioned for a repeal of the orders, alleging that the Crown had no such exclusive legislative power in Jersey, on the ground that Jersey had neither been conquered nor settled, and that even if the King had had such a right in John's time, that king had divested himself and his successors of it for

[1] See especially, 8 *State Trials,* N. S., pp. 311, 312, 314-316, and appendices B and C (pp. 1097-1126, 1127-1222), where reference is made to both sources and modern books and cases; also Renton and Phillimore, *Colonial Laws and Courts* (1907), pp. 128-142; William Forsyth, *Cases and Opinions on Constitutional Law* (1869), pp. 390-393; Sir Henry Jenkyns, *British Rule and Jurisdiction Beyond the Seas* (1902), pp. 37-41; Sir William R. Anson, *The Law and Custom of the Constitution,* vol. ii, Part II (3rd edition) chap. v, Section 2.

[2] *In the Matter of the States of Jersey,* 9 Moore; *Privy Council Cases,* 185 (1853); also in *State Trials,* New Series, 8, 285.

all time. On consideration of this petition of the
States and a petition against them signed by certain
citizens of Jersey, the Judicial Committee reported to
the Queen that although these orders appeared suit-
able for the improvement of the judicial administration in Jersey, "yet, as serious doubts exist whether
the establishment of such provisions by your Majesty's
prerogative without the assent of the States of *Jersey*
is consistent with the constitutional rights of the island,
their Lordships have agreed to report their opinion to
your Majesty to revoke the said Orders."[1] The orders were thereupon revoked by a subsequent order in
council, and some provisions of the Jersey States dealing with the same matters, but in a different way, were
ordered to be registered in Jersey, and this was done.

This was certainly a wise decision, but it does not
tend to weaken our suspicion of the historical correctness of these "serious doubts." This opinion was in
fact a tremendous admission, for it tolerated at least
a question as to the legitimacy of any legislative power
over Jersey of any sort. If the Crown had no such
power, there was, of course, no shadow of a claim for
Parliament; Jersey was at most clearly not a "dominion of the Crown," but only of the King. In 1861
precisely the same principle was followed in regard to

[1] 9 Moore *P. C.*, p. 262.

Guernsey in a case in which the Home Secretary had modified the local judicial machinery without consent of the States, and on complaint by them the Judicial Committee advised that the old arrangements should be revived, which was done.[1]

Since that time several other similar cases have come before the Judicial Committee.[2] In 1891, the States of Jersey petitioned against the execution of a royal warrant of pardon without previous registration in the Royal Court of Jersey, on which the Judicial Committee in their report evaded the direct constitutional issue.[3]

In the same year an order in council was made giving directions with reference to the appointment of a chairman of the Prison Board of Jersey. This order was presented to the Jersey Royal Court for registration, who suspended registration on the ground that this order was a modification of a former order made with the concurrence of the States, and referred the matter to the States, who in turn petitioned the Council to withdraw the second order because the Crown was not competent to legislate for Jersey without con-

---

[1] *In the Matter of the Petition of the States of Guernsey,* 14 Moore, *P. C.,* p. 368.

[2] 8 *State Trials,* N. S., pp. 314-316.

[3] *In Re Daniel.* This case is unreported, but a summary is given in 8 *State Trials,* N. S., pp. 314-315.

currence of the States, and because the second order was in violation of the earlier order in which the States had concurred. In 1894 this petition was considered, though counsel were limited in their arguments to the second point alone, and in pursuance of the report the objectionable second order was recalled by a subsequent order in council of June 27, 1894.[1]

It has long been the custom in the Channel Islands, for the Royal Court of Jersey or of Guernsey to register all legislation for the respective islands, whether of the Council or of Parliament, and it is the contention of the islanders that this registration is necessary before any such legislation, either of Parliament or of the Council, is binding in the islands. This assertion has been officially denied in England, but the view has never been relinquished by the islanders themselves.

In 1899 Sir Henry Jenkyns wrote, "The Channel Islands indeed claim to have conquered England, and are the sole fragments of the dukedom of Normandy which still continue attached to the British Crown. For this reason, in these islands alone of all British possessions, does any doubt arise as to whether an Act of the imperial Parliament is of its own force binding law."[2]

---

[1] 8 *State Trials,* N. S., pp. 315-316.
[2] *British Rule and Jurisdiction Beyond the Seas* (1902), p. 37.

In 1908 the late Sir William Anson wrote on this question, "It is maintained that no Order in Council may be put in force until it has been presented to the Royal Court for registration; that such registration may be suspended if the Order infringes the ancient laws and privileges of the Island: and further that the making of an Order in Council without the concurrence of the States is an infringement of these privileges.

"I will not pronounce upon a question which a Committee of the Privy Council have recently evaded. It is sufficient to say that the rights of the Crown are asserted, and that they are contested except as regards the exercise of the prerogative of mercy." [1]

In 1908 also appeared Mr. Fisher's constitutional interpretation of the American Revolution, according to which "To suppose that there was any part of the Empire to which the whole power of Parliament did not extend was as absurd to an Englishman in 1774 as it is today." [2]

Our conclusions as to the true constitutional relations of the realm to the dominions must be influenced

---

[1] *The Law and Custom of the Constitution,* vol. ii, Part II (third edition, 1908), p. 55.

[2] Sydney George Fisher, *The Struggle for American Independence* (1908), pp. 202-203; ante p.

by the consideration of another type of evidence,
namely, the views generally accepted and approved by
the courts of the reciprocal bond by which the King
and his subjects in or out of the realm were held to
their respective duties of protection and obedience—
the true nature of allegiance—another subject of considerable obscurity and difficulty. Possibly the best
approach to such a subject is through an examination
of *Calvin's Case,* which in many respects is a case of
first impression. In 1608 when the celebrated case
of the *Post-nati* was determined, two opposing views
existed on this subject: the older strictly feudal view,
sanctioned by a majority of the judges in the case itself, under which the subjects' allegiance was held to
be due solely to the natural person of the King without
regard to his office in the body politic of any particular realm; and a newer view, the result of the later development of the national and constitutional state, according to which allegiance was to the "body politic"
of the King, not to his natural person, and an allegiance therefore which was "tied to the law" of the
realm of which he was king. Thus Doddridge, one of
the ablest lawyers of his day, and others, urged in
support of the latter view, among other things, "that
'lex et ligeancia' came out of one root, and as it is
called 'lex a ligando,' so it is called 'legeance, a liga-

tione'; which proveth allegiance to be tied to laws;
and consequently the laws of these two nations [Eng-
land and Scotland] being several, notwithstanding the
union of sovereignty in the king's person, the allegiance of the subjects remaineth still several";[1] and
further, "that *regnum* and *rex* were relatives, and
therefore distinct kingdoms, distinct kings as to the
kingdoms; and the person of the king possessing both
kingdoms possesseth the people and the laws of them
distinct, as the kingdoms are themselves. Therefore
the subjection of every people is distinguished to the
several kingdoms, and one not subject to the other,
nor naturalized within the other."[2] Against this interpretation was arrayed the combined strength of
Coke, Bacon, and Ellesmere. One extract from Ellesmere must suffice: "But touching the severall lawes;
I say, that severall lawes can make no difference in
matter of soveraigntie; and in the bond of allegiance
and obedience to one king . . . for where there is
but one sovereigne, all his subjects borne in all his dominions bee borne *ad fidem regis;* and are bound to
him by one bond of faith and allegiance; and in that,
one is not greater nor lesser than an other; nor one to
bee preferred before another, but all to bee obedient

---

[1] *Howell's State Trials,* ii, column 567.
[2] *Howell's State Trials,* ii, column 568.

alike; and to be ruled alike; yet under severall lawes and customes." [1]

Theoretically it would be a nice question to decide between these two conflicting points of view. On feudal theory the second was unquestionable, and many things were yet feudal in England at the opening of the seventeenth century. On the other hand the whole structure of the English national state had developed at the expense of feudalism in the centuries since the Conquest, and the King had become really *rex* rather than feudal *dominus,* the head of a national state, with certain rights in his office guaranteed to his successors as well as himself by the *jus coronae.* But Parliament, rightly or wrongly, had declared James I King by hereditary right, *i.e.,* by the feudal rules of succession, [2] and the judges now declared in *Calvin's Case* that allegiance to him was not national but personal. Whatever the merit of the national view may have been— and it was considerable—the doctrine of English law was established by *Calvin's Case* in 1608, and established clearly and beyond question, and this before any permanent plantations of Englishmen, except Jamestown, had been made in America. The allegiance which binds a subject to his sovereign seems under

---

[1] *Ibid.,* column 684. The whole case should be read.
[2] 1 Jac. 1, cap. 1.

that case to require no obedience to the laws of any of that sovereign's dominion beyond the one of which that subject is a member. The post-natal Scots were not subject to English laws or an English parliament. They were subject only to the King and their own laws and parliament, but they had the rights of Englishmen.

This might well seem conclusive for Ireland and all other dominions of the King as well. On its face it establishes a firm constitutional basis for the claims of Darcy for Ireland in 1641, and of Samuel Adams for America in 1773. But on the reasoning followed, no warrant clearly appears for a restriction of the principle of *Calvin's Case* merely to the *post-nati*. Why should it not be extended to the *ante-nati* as well? Prudential reasons no doubt led to the careful suppression of all consideration of the latter in 1608, but it was too important a question long to lie dormant.[1]

---

[1] The relations between England and Scotland were a delicate political as well as legal question in 1608. The English Parliament reflected the English hostility to the Scots, and had lately refused to pass the bill fully carrying out James's favorite scheme of a union of the two countries. (*Parliamentary History,* vol. i, pp. 1018-1023, 1075-1119; Gardiner, *History of England,* vol. i, pp. 324-337.) It was therefore desirable to introduce no more into the decision in *Calvin's Case* than was absolutely necessary. There was a legal reason also that increased the delicacy of the question. The *ante-nati* might possibly be excluded if the prince to whom they had previously owed allegiance had been totally

In the case of *Craw* v. *Ramsay*, 21 and 22 Charles
II, this question was elaborately discussed in the Court

independent feudally of the King of England before he himself
ascended the English throne.   On the other hand, it was the
doctrine of the law that these Scottish subjects might inherit in
England, "If they be born subjects to a Prince, holding his Kingdom or Territories as Homager and Liegeman to the King of
England, during the time of his being Homager."   (*Craw v.
Ramsay, Vaughan's Reports,* p. 281.)   But it was notorious that
since the time of Edward I the English had constantly insisted
that the Kingdom of Scotland was held as a fief of the King of
England and the Scottish King his "homager."   (The references
are set out at length by Selden in his notes to Fortescue's *De
Laudibus Legum Angliæ,* chapter xiii, pp. 5-6, London 1660.)
This was, of course, as strenuously denied by the Scots, and Sir
Thomas Craig, the author of the *De Unione Regnorum,* wrote a
book in 1602 to disprove it (*Scotland's Soveraignty Asserted,*
London, 1695; the Latin original was never printed), possibly not
without royal encouragement.   As late as Elizabeth's reign a
Scot accused of rape had been denied a trial *per mediatatem linguæ*
in England, "because a Scot was never here accounted an alien, but
rather a subject."   (Dyer's Reports, p. 304a.)   Clearly this was
a nice question legally and an exceedingly dangerous one politically.   One may well doubt whether the exclusion of the *ante-nati*
was sound law.   The reason was political.

The whole history of treason is a commentary upon the central
principle of *Calvin's Case* that allegiance is personal and not national.   There is much of value on the earlier and contemporary
views of this matter in Sir Matthew Hale's *History of the Pleas
of the Crown;* Sir Edward Coke's *Institutes, First, Second* and
Third; Hawkins, *Pleas of the Crown,* Sir Michael Foster's *Crown
Law;* Stanford, *Pleas of the Crown;* Lord Chancellor West's
Discourse Concerning Treasons; Sir Robert Holbourne's *Reading
on the Statute of Treason,* and the many trials for treason reported in the *State Trials.*   In Strafford's Case, St. John made a
strong plea for the theory that treason could be committed

of Common Pleas on an action of ejectment.[1] Robert
Ramsay, Scot and *ante-natus,* had four sons, all *ante-
nati.* Of these the eldest died leaving no male issue.
John, the third son, was naturalised by the English
Parliament and acquired land in England, but died
without issue. George, the fourth son, was naturalised by act of the English Parliament and his grand-
son, the eldest son of his eldest son, the present defendant, claimed the lands of John in his right. Nich-
olas, the second son, was never naturalised by the English Parliament but came under the operation of the
act of the Irish Parliament in 10 Charles I, by which
all the Scottish *ante-nati* were naturalised in the Kingdom of Ireland. Soon after this naturalisation, Patrick, his only son, was born, and the plaintiff in this
case claims under a title derived through several trans-
fers from him.

There are several points material to the case but the
only one important for us is, "Whether a naturaliza-
tion in Ireland will naturalize the person in England?
If it will not, all other Questions are out of the Case."[2]

---

against the politic person of the King (Rushworth, Strafford's
Trial, pp. 694ff) ; but his argument apparently failed to convince
the Lords. Pym's Argument to the same effect—strikingly in-
conclusive—is in Rushworth, *op. cit.,* p. 661ff.

[1] *Vaughan's Reports,* 274ff.

[2] *Ibid.,* p. 277.

This is a fundamental and far reaching issue. It involved the questions whether under the law of England and the doctrine of Calvin's case, an *ante-natus* of Scotland can inherit lands in England, and second, if not, whether he acquires such a right through naturalisation by the Parliament of Ireland. If either of these questions were answered in the affirmative, the second son might inherit under the law of primogeniture; if in the negative, the fourth son, heir at law to one naturalised by the English Parliament, would inherit instead.

This clearly raises a question that affects the status of all the King's dominions and the rights of the inhabitants of the whole, and involves the fundamental conception of the nature of fealty. In the end the court was divided, Chief Justice Vaughan and Justice Tyrrell for the plaintiff, Wylde and Archer for the defendant, and the report is far from clear in many points,[1] but the bulk of the argument closely touches the central problem of the Empire on which the American Revolution also turns, and the plantations are explicitly brought in. I have stated the material facts of the case at a length seemingly undue, because it is

[1] These reports were published after Sir John Vaughan's death by his son, and some of the cases are clearly in the form of rather rough notes.

clear from them that here two of the four judges of
the Court of Common Pleas, including Chief Justice
Vaughan himself, must have accepted the theory that
the Irish Parliament had authority to naturalise an
alien in England, a concession of considerable significance for our purpose.

The arguments themselves are rather confusedly
reported and their tendency is apparently against the
conclusion of Vaughan, who reports the case, all of
which adds to our difficulty, but many particular statements are of great importance. It was said, for example, that "Ireland then differs from Scotland, in a
common difference with Gernsey, Jersey, Isle of Man,
Berwick, and all the English Plantations, for that they
are Dominions belonging to the Crown of England,
which Scotland is not." [1]

"By the Doctrine of Calvin's Case, a natural born
subject to the King's person of a Forraign Dominion,
is not privileged in England from being an Alien, else
the *Antenati* of Scotland were priviledg'd, for they are
natural born Subjects to the King's person, as well as
the *Postnati*." "It stands not with the Resolution of
that Case, That the natural born Subjects of the Dominions belonging to the Crown of England (qua

---

[1] *Vaughan's Reports*, p. 278.

such) should be no Aliens in England, which was the principal matter to have been discuss'd, but was not, in Calvin's Case, and chiefly concerns the point in question. . . .

"What Inference could be made for the Resolution of Calvin's Case? That because the King's natural Subjects of Dominions belonging to the Crown of England, as these did, [*i. e.,* inhabitants of Normandy, Anjou, Calais, Jersey, Ireland, etc., relied on in the decision in Calvin's case] were no Aliens in England: Therefore that Subjects of a Dominion not belonging to the Crown, as the *Postnati* of Scotland are, should be no Aliens in England, *Non Sequitur.*

"Therefore it is for another reason then, because natural Subjects of Dominions belonging to the Crown of England, they were no Aliens by the meaning of that Resolution. . . .

"It was not because they were natural Subjects of him that was King of England, for then the *Antenati* of Scotland would be no aliens. . . .

"It was not because they were natural subjects of Dominions belonging to the Crown of England; for then the *Postnati* would be Aliens in England. . . .

"It remains then, the Reason can be no other, but because they were born under the same Liegeance with

the Subjects of England, which is the direct reason
of that Resolution in Calvin's Case . . .

"The time of his birth is chiefly to be considered,
for he cannot be a Subject born of one Kingdom, that
was born under the Liegeance of a King of another
Kingdom, albeit afterwards one Kingdom descend to
the King of the other."[1]

Against this it was urged that "A person naturalized in England is the same as if he had been born in
England, and a person naturalized in Ireland is the
same as if he had been born in Ireland.

"But a person born in Ireland is the same as if he
had been born, or naturalized in England.

"Therefore a person naturalized in Ireland, is the
same as if he had been born or naturalized in England."[2]   The answer was that by similar reasoning
Scots naturalised in Scotland after the Union would be
no aliens in England, but aliens they were.   "Therefore the same Conclusion should be made of one naturalized in Ireland."[3]

"Another Objection, subtile enough, is, That if naturalizing in Ireland, which makes a man as born there,

---

[1] *Vaughan's Reports*, pp. 285-287.
[2] *Ibid.*, p. 287.
[3] *Ibid.*

shall not make him likewise as born (that is no Alien)' in England, That then naturalizing in England should not make a man no Alien in Ireland (especially without naming Ireland). . . .

"The inference is not right in form, nor true. The Answer is, The People of England now do, and always did, consist of Native Persons, Naturaliz'd Persons, and Denizen'd Persons; and no people, of what consistence soever they be, can be Aliens to that they have conquer'd by Arms, or otherwise subjected to themselves, (for it is a contradiction to be a stranger to that which is a mans own, and against common reason and publique practise)."[1]

"Though Ireland have its own Parliament, yet it is not absolute & *sui juris,* for if it were, England had no power over it, and it were as free after Conquest and Subjection by England, as before.'

"Ireland is a distinct Kingdom from England, and therefore cannot make any Law Obligative to England.

"That is no adequate Reason, for by that Reason England being a distinct Kingdom, should make no law to bind Ireland, which is not so: England can naturalize, if it please, nominally a person in Ireland, and not in England. But he recover'd by saying, That

---

[1] *Vaughan's Reports,* p. 291.
[2] *Ibid.,* p. 292.

Ireland was subordinate to England, and therefore could not make a Law Obligatory to England. True; for every Law is coactive, and it is contradiction that the Inferior, which is civilly the lesser power, should compel the Superior, which is greater power.

"Secondly, He said England and Ireland were two distinct Kingdoms, and no otherwise united than because they had one Soveraign. Had this been said of Scotland and England, it had been right, for they are both absolute Kingdoms, and each of them *Sui Juris*.

"But Ireland far otherwise; For it is a Dominion belonging to the Crown of England, and follows that it cannot be separate from it, but by Act of Parliament of England, no more than Wales, Gernsey, Jersey, Barwick, the English Plantations, all which are Dominions belonging to the Realm of England, though not within the Territorial Dominion or Realm of England, but follow it, and are a part of its Royalty.

Thirdly, That distinct Kingdoms cannot be united, but by mutual Acts of Parliament. True; if they be Kingdoms *Sui Juris,* and independent upon each other; as England and Scotland cannot be united but by reciprocal Acts of Parliament. . . .

"But Wales, after the Conquest of it by Edward the First, was annext to England, *Jure Proprietatis.*
. . . .

"Ireland in nothing differs from it, but in having a Parliament, *Gratia Regis,* subject to the Parliament of England, it might have had so, if the King pleas'd; but it was annext to England. None doubts Ireland, as conquer'd, as it; and as much subject to the Parliament of England, if it please." [1]

The interest of this case lies in the distinction drawn between dominions *of the Crown* of England, of which Ireland was one, as well as Jersey, and the plantations; and dominions *of the King* of England, like Scotland. Some such distinction was necessary to justify the denial of the rights of subjects in England to the *Ante-nati.* From this the inference was drawn that dominions of the Crown, though not those of the King, are subordinate to the Realm, and subject to the English Parliament, while any parliaments they themselves may have are subordinate and incapable of enacting law for England. The linking of Ireland and Ireland's parliament with the plantations and their assemblies as "dominions of the Crown," is interesting, whatever we may think of the strength of the reasoning on which it is based. The difficulty was all due to the exclusion of the *Ante-nati.* The distinction of Dominions of the King and Dominions of the Crown

---

[1] *Vaughan's Reports,* pp. 299-301.

is created by that, and upon that distinction rightly or wrongly a subordination to the English Parliament is assumed to exist in all Dominions of the Crown; but whether the original distinction is really consistent with the opinions of Coke and Ellesmere and Bacon in Calvin's Case might be open to considerable doubt.

If the Despencers' distinction between King and Crown in Edward II's day is "damnable and damned" as Coke said in Calvin's Case, it is hard to see just how a distinction between Dominions of the King and Dominions of the Crown could have much hope of salvation, or why the gates of the Kingdom should be ajar for *post-nati* but fast closed to *ante-nati*. And if there be no real difference between dominions, how can a subordination to Parliament be justified in one which is admitted not to exist in another? "I believe," says Professor Maitland, "that an habitual and perfectly unambiguous personification of the Crown—in particular, the attribution of acts to the Crown—is much more modern than most people would believe. It seems to me that in fully half the cases in which Sir William Anson writes 'Crown,' Blackstone would have written 'King.' In strictness, however, 'the Crown' is not, I take it, among the persons known to our law, unless it is merely another name for the King. The Crown, by that name, never sues, never prose-

cutes, never issues writs or letters patent.   On the face
of formal records the King or Queen does it all." [1]
One may surmise that Vaughan too had some doubts
about it.   He and one more of the four judges of the
Court of Common Pleas at least conceded to the Irish
Parliament a power of naturalising for the Kingdom
of England, since they had admitted that if it had none,
all other questions were "out of the Case" of *Craw
v. Ramsay,* and yet both held for the plaintiff in that
case.   Whether justifiable or not, however, this distinction between King and Crown was to play a considerable part in the future development of the constitutional problem of the Empire.

The consideration of fealty in general, and of the
definitions and discussions of it in Calvin's Case and
Craw v. Ramsay seem to me to tend on the whole to
strengthen Ireland's claim to local legislative auton-
omy, particularly when the precedents of the Channel
Islands are combined with the Irish in determining
the status of the dominions outside the realm, among
which the plantations must be included.

The chief argument for Irish dependence to be
found in these cases—one, by the way, not applicable
to the Channel Islands nor to the majority of the
American colonies—arises from Coke's assertion *obiter*

---

[1] *The Crown as Corporation, Collected Papers,* vol. iii, p. 257.

in Calvin's Case that Ireland was really conquered by
the English in the twelfth century. This assertion
was strenuously and elaborately denied by Molyneux,
who strove to prove that English rule was volun-
tarily received and not imposed by force. He further
denied that even conquest could confer a permanent
right of domination. This question has less importance for America than for Ireland, and for further
consideration of it I must refer the reader to Molyneux's *Case Stated* and Atwood's Reply.[1]

---

[1] Most of the American pamphleteers who made any use of the
Irish constitutional parallel admitted that Ireland was a conquered country, but denied that America was, and on this difference they based a superior claim to an independence of the English Parliament. For example, James Wilson, in his *Considerations,* written in 1774 (Works of James Wilson, 1804), vol. iii, p.
234; Dickinson's *Essay,* of the same year (Philadelphia, 1774),
p. 389, and others, but particularly John Adams, who in the ninth
and tenth parts of the papers of *Novanglus* goes into the most
elaborate examination of this point. "The authority of parliament to bind Ireland at all, if it has any, is founded upon entirely a
different principle from any that takes place in the case of
America. It is founded on the consent and compact of the Irish
by Poyning's law to be so governed, if it have any foundation at
all; and this consent was given, and compact made, in consequence of a conquest." (*Works,* 1851, vol. iv, p. 151). "These
are the principles upon which the dependence and subordination of
Ireland are founded. Whether they are just or not is not necessary for us to inquire. The Irish nation have never been entirely
convinced of their justice, have been never discontented with
them, and ripe and ready to dispute them. Their reasonings have
ever been answered by the *ratio ultima* and *penultima* of the
tories." (*Ibid.,* p. 158.) "After all, I believe there is no evi-

But whether conquered or not, all "dominions of the
Crown" had after 1641 practically, if not in right,
become a part of "the Commonwealth of England and

---

dence of any express contract of the Irish nation, to be governed
by the English parliament, and very little of an implied one:
that the notion of binding it by acts in which it is expressly
named is merely arbitrary; and that this nation, which has ever
had many and great virtues, has been most grievously oppressed.
And it is to this day so greatly injured and oppressed, that I
wonder American committees of correspondence and congresses
have not attended more to it than they have. Perhaps in some
future time they may." (*Ibid.*, p. 165.) "But thus much is certain, that none of these principles take place in America. She
never was conquered by Britain. She never consented to be a
state dependent upon, or subordinate to the British parliament,
excepting only in the regulation of her commerce." (*Ibid.*, p.
158.) "It [America] came not to the king by descent, but was
explored by the settlers. It came not by marriage to the king,
but was purchased by the settlers of the savages." (*Ibid.*, p.
170.) Even New York he considers not to be a real conquest,
for the Dutch title was never valid.

Since conquest was the only ground that could be alleged in
Calvin's Case and *Craw* v. *Ramsay,* for a difference between the
status of Scotland and Ireland, this insistence upon the absence
of any right derived from conquest in America is the more
important.

For further references to conquest, and the difference in status
between conquered and settled colonies, see especially in addition to the cases already referred to, Sir John Davis' Reports,
London 1628, folio 28, *Le Case de Tanistry* (in English, Dublin,
1762, *The Case of Tanistry,* p. 78), in 5 James I, for Ireland;
Dutton v. *Howell, Shower's Cases in Parliament,* London, 1698,
p. 24, about 1689, for Barbadoes; *Blankard* v. *Galdy,* 2 *Salkeld's
Reports,* 411, 5 William and Mary, for Jamaica; *Rex.* v. *Cowle,
Burrow's Reports,* ii, 834, in 1759, for Berwick on Tweed, especially the opinion of Lord Mansfield; *Campbell* v. *Hall, Howell's*

the dominions and territories thereunto belonging,"
as they were officially termed after 1649, and they
were treated as such by the English Parliament and
government, just as much and just as soon as necessity
seemed to demand. For Ireland, Molyneux was answered by the Declaratory Act of 1719 which arose
out of the immediate question of judicial appeals,[1]

State Trials, vol. xx, 239, in 1774, for the Island of Grenada,
especially Lord Mansfield's opinion and the criticisms of Baron
Masères added by the editor; Also, *A Discoverie of the True
Causes why Ireland was never entirely Subdued, nor brought
under Obedience of the Crowne of England,* by Sir John Davis
(James I's Attorney General in Ireland), London, 1747; Sir
Matthew Hale, *The History of the Common Law of England*
(London, 1820), chapters 9-10, with the valuable notes of the
editor, Sergeant Charles Runnington; Blackstone's *Commentaries,*
Introduction, Section IV (*Of the Countries Subject to the Laws
of England*); *Cases and Opinions on Constitutional Law,* by
William Forsyth, London, 1869, especially the note to chapter
one (p. 12ff), 333ff, and 391-393; *Constitutional Law,* by Her-
bert Broom, second edition, London, 1885, pp. 3-56; William
Burge, *Commentaries on Colonial and Foreign Laws,* or the
reprint of a part of it edited by Renton and Phillimore with the
title, *Colonial Laws and Courts,* London, 1907; Tarring, C. J.,
The Law Relating to the Colonies, fourth edition, London, 1913.

[1] Extracts from the *Lords' Journals* dealing with the judicial
issue that resulted in the Act of 1719 are given in John Mac-
queen's *House of Lords and Privy Council Practice,* London,
1842, Appendix, No. v, pp. 787-791. Curiously enough, in the
third article of the charge against the Earl of Strafford in 1641,
he was alleged to be guilty of treason because he had declared
"that Ireland was a conquered nation and that the King might do
with them what he pleased (Rushworth, Straffords' Trial, p. 155).
There was a good deal of argument in this celebrated case on

and this declaration was followed up by a practical exercise of Parliament's power in a long series of acts that extended to 1780. For America the exercise of a similar power by Parliament began with the Navigation Act of 1651 and was continued after the Restoration and Revolution in a series of acts restraining trade and manufactures, too well known to need repetition here. Not until the close of the Seven Years' War, however, and the Stamp Act resulting from it, did the Americans feel the full weight of the theory of the imperial commonwealth as set up by the Long Parliament. And as this act happened to be an exercise of taxing power the Americans in opposing it were at first content to rely on the narrower claim of Parliament's inability only to levy a tax. They erected a statue to a statesman who while derying Parliament's power to tax would have asserted its unlimited author-

---

this and other points not unconnected with our subject. See, for example, Rushworth, *op. cit.*, pp. 457, 640-641, 662. Among other things, Pym, St. John and Glyn took up the whole question of the relation of the English Parliament and the English laws to Ireland (pp. 690-691, 693, 694-699, 711), and also the jurisdiction of the English Parliament in cases of treason alleged to be committed in Ireland (694-699). The last point is interesting because it touches the issue upon which the Declaratory Act of 1719 for Ireland was passed. The most important precedent was the case of Lord Leonard Grey in the reign of Henry VIII, of which some account is given in *Howell's State Trials I,* 439, with a valuable prefatory note by Francis Hargrave.

ity to bind and restrain in every other respect whatsoever. Otis, it is true, in opposing the writs of assistance in 1761, and later in his *Rights of the Colonies,*
had taken broader ground and had ventured to apply
the words "unconstitutional" to other than revenue
acts and to deny Parliament's right to enact them, but
in this he had relied on natural right or fundamental
law, rather than on the constitutional distinction between the realm and the King's other dominions with
which alone we are at present directly concerned. The
Declaratory Act of 1766 which accompanied the repeal
of the Stamp Act, of course, was passed over the bit-
terest opposition of Pitt and Camden, but their opposition was due solely to the inclusion in the declaration
of the Parliament's right to tax. Pitt, at least, was in
heartiest accord with its sweeping assumption of power
in every other respect. There is nothing to indicate
that he was not in fullest sympathy with the constitutional theory that Molyneux had attacked. As Mr.
Hertz[1] and Miss Hotblack[2] have shown, Pitt's political
horizon was limited to the prevailing narrow economic
doctrines of his day; he was content with a British
Empire that would impose a permanent barrier to the
ambitious designs of French domination, though he

---

[1] *The Old Colonial System,* by G. B. Hertz, Manchester, 1905.
[2] *Chatham's Colonial Policy,* by Kate Hotblack, London, 1917.

was far in advance of most contemporary Englishmen in seeing that this could never be done in Europe alone. Constitutionally likewise, he was enlightened beyond the general level of his time in recognising that the British Empire could never impose such a barrier unless the loyalty of the colonies was secured by the necessary concession of the right of consent to taxation for support of internal government. But politically he never had a glimpse of the true character of the British Empire as it has developed in the nineteenth century, and constitutionally he was fully convinced of the right and duty of the English Parliament to bind and rule all outside dominions in all matters whatsover with the single exception of levying a tax for support of government without consent of the taxed. There was much in common between him and Galloway, and even Dickinson; but from Molyneux and John and Samuel Adams he was poles apart. The American victory in securing the repeal of the Stamp Act could furnish no final solution because it did not touch the fundamental question, the real relation of the English Parliament and the dominions, or the assumption of 1649 that the English Commonwealth, including all the dominions, was really one and indivisible, and to be ruled absolutely by a Parliament of the English nation, the central constitutional problem

of British imperialism from 1640 to the present day.
This was seen clearly enough in the Parliament itself
in the debates upon the repeal and the Declaratory
Act, and in the enactment of the latter in the same
uncompromising form as the act of 1719 binding Ireland. In the colonies, too, the practical enforcement
of the principles of this Act under the doctrinaire leadership of Grenville and Townshend soon convinced
some of the leading statesmen that a settled design
existed in England "to enslave America,"[1] and that
their own resistance must continue till they obtained
a full recognition of the principle that the whole of
England's legislative authority ended at the low-water
line. Lack of space makes impossible here a detailed
tracing of the growing perception in America of the
necessity for this wider ground of opposition. It has
been done many times. A few striking contemporary
statements must suffice as illustrations of it. The Massachusetts Circular Letter of 1768[2] is a great advance
beyond the principles of the Stamp Act Congress of

[1] *Resolutions of the Towns of Suffolk County, Massachusetts,* at
Milton, September 6th, 1774, *Journals of the Continental Congress,*
Ford's edition, vol. i, p. 33.

[2] Alden Bradford, *Speeches of the Governors of Massachusetts,
from 1765 to 1775, and the Answers of the House of Representatives, with their Resolutions,* pp. 134-136. This is conveniently
reprinted in William MacDonald, *Select Charters,* p. 330ff, and
his *Documentary Source Book,* p. 146ff. See *Post,* p. 156ff.

1765. The authors of that letter have passed beyond an opposition to the mere exercise of legislative power in taxation to the wider principles of the validity of that power itself, but they have not yet reached the final and the firmest ground of opposition to it; they still rely solely on the contention of Camden that it is an "unalterable right, in nature, engrafted into the British constitution, as a fundamental law," that taxation must only be with the consent of the taxed. There was no stopping here, however. In 1774 the so-called First Continental Congress made what may be considered the first official statement of the final and fundamental constitutional position of the American opposition. It appears in the *Resolutions,* adopted by the Congress on October 14, 1774.[1] In the original draft, prepared by Major John Sullivan, the principle is set forth in the following form: "That the power of making laws for ordering or regulating the internal polity of these Colonies, is, within the limits of each Colony, respectively and exclusively vested in the Provincial Legislature of such Colony; and that all statutes for ordering or regulating the internal polity of the said Colonies, or any of them, in any manner, or in any case whatsoever, are illegal and void."[2]

[1] *Journals of the Continental Congress* (Ford), vol. i, p. 63ff.
[2] *Ibid.,* p. 67.

In its final form, as adopted by the Congress, this appears as article four of the *Declaration,* and the changes were mainly due to John Adams.[1]   It was adopted only after a prolonged and bitter opposition led by Galloway, and is as follows:

"That the foundation of English liberty, and of all free government, is a right in the people to participate in their legislative council; and as the English colonists are not represented, and from their local and other circumstances, cannot properly be represented in the British parliament, they are entitled to a free and exclusive power of legislation in their several provincial legislatures, where their right of representation can alone be preserved, in all cases of taxation and internal polity, subject only to the negative of their sovereign, in such manner as has been heretofore used and accustomed. But, from the necessity of the case, and a regard to the mutual interest of both countries, we cheerfully consent to the operation of such acts of the British parliament, as are bona fide, restrained to the regulation of our external commerce, for the purpose of securing the commercial advantages of the whole empire to the mother country, and the commercial benefits of its respective members; excluding every idea of taxation, internal or external, for raising a

[1] *Ibid.,* p. 63.

revenue on the subjects in America, without their consent." [1]

In the petition to the King adopted in the Congress on October 26th, England is referred to as "that nation" with which the colonists have been in contention, and the statement is made that "We wish not a diminution of the prerogative." [2]   In this famous article four, the essential constitutional claim of America is presented with all clearness.   There is the fullest acceptance of the royal prerogative coupled with the most definite denial of the constitutional authority of the Parliament of the "nation" of England in any way to legislate for the American dominions, while an exception is made in matters of general imperial trade, but one expressly declared to be not of right but only by way of voluntary concession.   Legally Parliament possesses no power of legislation for the colonies, practically it may exercise such powers by consent except in matters of "internal polity."   In this phrase "internal polity" occurs for aught I know, the first approximation formally made of the working compromise by which the "self-governing colonies" have been so successfully held within the new British Empire which arose on the ruins of the old colonial system.   It is

---

[1] *Journals*, vol. i, pp. 68-69.
[2] *Ibid.*, vol. i, p. 119.

an approximation only, though a close one, for the Declaratory Act of 1768 still stands unrepealed in law, for internal as well as external matters; but the long continued habit of a non-exercise of these powers in matters of "internal polity" may now properly be called a "convention of the constitution" if not a law. "The legislative supremacy of Parliament over the whole of the British dominions is complete and undoubted in law, though for constitutional or practical reasons, Parliament abstains from exercising that supreme legislative power."[1]

Thus the Congress in 1774 really furnished the formula, and apparently for the first time formally, under which the British Empire of self-governing colonies has become possible, an empire absolutely unique in its working and structure in the history of the world.

In the modern Empire the Parliament claims a paramount right but concedes that it shall not be put in practice except in imperial matters. Adams claimed a total exemption of right, but conceded an exception to this in practice in matters imperial and not of mere "internal polity." The one is the converse of the other, but the general principle is identical. The identity, however, is in the practical result only. In strict

---

[1] Sir Henry Jenkyns, *British Rule and Jurisdiction Beyond the Seas*, p. 10.

law the two solutions are as far apart as the contentions of Molyneux and Mansfield. The rigorous logic
of his theory of sovereignty compelled Mansfield to demand one ultimate and undivided authority and he
could brook no exception even of a practical kind.
Adams had a somewhat similar legal theory, except
that the seat of authority must be in the colony itself,
and he would have made concessions in practice. Both
views were in effect Austinian. But Austinianism is
logic, and logic is not all of life. So, happily, an illogical modern Empire has arisen not unlike the modern
limited monarchy for the realm itself, in defiance of
Austin and in the teeth of Lord John Russell's repetition of Mansfield's dictum: no dependence, no sovereignty; with its futile logic, always so soothing to
the timid souls who live in constant dread of surren-
dering their "sovereignty" to somebody or other. For
Lord Mansfield, the sovereignty of the Parliament and
the dependency of the dominions must continue to co-
exist. They must stand or fall together. In truth
they must, under the old definitions, and if all the results of the English Revolution are accepted as legitimate. But times have changed since 1688, and it is not
too much to hope that some day the theory too will
change; for theory after all is expected at least to ap-
proximate fact, though it matters little whether this

change is effected by law or merely by convention. But Adams, Austinian though in a certain sense he was, looked further into the future, and saw what Mansfield could not, that for a working empire his theory must be modified in practice by a voluntary concession. Such a compromise, however, was too advanced for the rigorous logic of the eighteenth century.

Happily this collision of law and fact, under the more fortunate circumstances of the new British Empire, with the disappearance of older vicious economic doctrines and the emergence of a milder temper among English statesmen, has had few serious results. In the eighteenth century neither of these should be expected and neither was found, and the divergence in law unmitigated by any alleviation in practice ultimately wrecked the old empire. The quarrel came at a time when on either side few men, like Adams, were yet able to look beyond the mere law and find a working solution in a practice which could leave untouched their mutually contradictory legal claims without making them a barrier to a peaceful association under the titular sovereignty of a common King.

It is our purpose here to assess if possible the merits of these opposing legal claims which brought on the crisis, and these alone.

Nevertheless, the underlying principle of law with concessions, though temporarily a failure, constitutes a signal proof, if proof were needed, of John Adams' political sagacity as well as his constitutional knowledge. For the successful working of this principle of the empire has depended essentially upon the preservation of this line of demarcation here asserted in 1774 between matters imperial and matters of "internal polity" in a colony. Such a line was in turn anticipated by Charles Buller and Lord Durham and Gibbon Wakefield in the epoch-making proposals of Lord Durham's *Report on Canada* in 1839 and in Charles Buller's report on the Canadian public lands preliminary to it. "I know not," said Lord Durham in the *Report,* "in what respect it can be desirable that we should interfere with their internal legislation in matters which do not affect their relations with the mother country. The matters, which so concern us, are very few. The constitution of the form of government,—the regulation of foreign relation, and of trade with the mother country, the other British Colonies, and foreign nations,—and the disposal of the public lands, are the only points on which the mother country requires a control." [1]

---

[1] *Lord Durham's Report on Canada,* London, 1902, p. 207. The inclusion of public lands, which the Americans would no doubt

Since the time when the Earl of Elgin, Lord Durham's son-in-law, first put these theories into actual practice in Canada, there has been a steady and constant shifting of this line between matters imperial and "internal legislation," and with the growth of the spirit of colonial nationalism this shift has always made for a greater and greater narrowing of the imperial sphere and a corresponding widening of the scope and extent of matters of "internal polity." First the lands were taken over, then immigration, taxation and defence; and in our own day there is a marked tendency to transfer even a part of "the regulation of foreign relation." In very recent years, the effects of the Great War and the resulting strong impulse towards a greater nationalism in the self-governing colonies have greatly accelerated a current which was already setting strongly in the direction of a nationalistic solution of the problem of empire, and away from the proposals for a new and closer constitutional

---

have repudiated in 1774, was due mainly to Buller's preliminary report on that subject. It is reprinted in volume iii of Sir C. P. Lucas's edition of the *Report* (Oxford, 1912), pp. 34-130. Buller was an enthusiastic supporter of the views of E. G. Wakefield as to the necessity for a careful control of public lands in new colonies and their sale at an "adequate" price. These views are set forth at length in Wakefield's *Art of Colonization*. See also, the *Life of Lord Durham,* by Stuart J. Reid, and *Self-Government in Canada,* by F. Bradshaw, London, 1903.

bond between the various parts of the empire, as proposed by the Imperialists. But wherever the actual line at any time may have been, it is the constant adherence at all times in practice to the principle that such a line does exist somewhere that has guaranteed the contentment and permanence of the British Empire for three-quarters of a century; and the first formal statement of this principle seems to have been the work of the first Continental Congress. John Adams deserves some place with Wakefield, Durham, Buller, Molesworth, and the other intellectual founders of the modern British Commonwealth of Nations.

But though the definite formal statement of this happy constitutional formula was probably not made till late in the year 1774, more than a year earlier than this there is to be found in Massachusetts a document—one of the most remarkable in the whole series of American "revolutionary" state papers—in which the historical and constitutional basis of article four of the *Declaration* is set forth with the greatest ingenuity and a thorough understanding of British constitutional development. This is the *Answer* given by the Massachusetts assembly on March 2, 1773, to a speech delivered to them by Governor Hutchinson on February 16th of the same year.[1]

---

[1] Both these remarkable papers are printed in Alden Bradford's

In his address Governor Hutchinson adverted to a previous important statement of the Assembly which I am obliged for lack of space to omit,[1] in which they had asserted "that the colonies were an acquisition of foreign territory, not annexed to the realm of England . . . that this was the sense of the English Crown, the nation, and our predecessors, when they first took possession of this country; that, if the colonies were not then annexed to the realm, they cannot have been since that time; that, if they are not now annexed to the realm, they are not part of the kingdom; and, consequently, not subject to the

---

Speeches of the Governors of Massachusetts, pp. 368-396. I take them for more convenient reference from the reprint in *The Principles and Acts of the Revolution,* by Hezekiah Niles, second edition, 1876. Hutchinson's Address is at page 79, the Answer follows at page 87.

[1] On the sixth of January, 1773, Hutchinson had addressed the House in the speech which seems to be one of the first definite official statements of the imperial problems in America. "I know of no line," he had said, "that can be drawn between the supreme authority of Parliament and the total independence of the colonies" (p. 340). The speech is printed in *Speeches of the Governors of Massachusetts from 1765 to 1775,* etc. (edited by Alden Bradford), Boston, 1818, pp. 336-342. On January 25, 1773, the address of the House, referred to above, was given in answer (Bradford, *Speeches,* pp. 342-351). It was prepared by a committee which included Samuel Adams. It is of great importance and flatly contradicts the governor's assertion, but the underlying constitutional issue is less explicitly stated than in the answer of a few weeks later from which, therefore, I have chosen to illustrate this point.

legislative authority of the kingdom; for no country, by the common law, was subject to the laws or to the parliament, but the realm of England."

"Now, if this foundation shall fail you in every part of it, as I think it will, the fabric which you have raised upon it must fall." [1]

"Let me then observe to you, that as English subjects, and agreeable to the doctrine of feudal tenure, all our lands and tenements are held mediately, or immediately, of the crown, and although the possession and use, or profits, be in the subject, there still remains a dominion in the crown . . . and whensoever any part of such territories, by grant from the crown, becomes the possession or property of private persons, such persons, thus holding, under the crown of England, remain, or become subjects of England, to all intents and purposes. . . . But that it is now, or was, when the plantations were first granted, the prerogative of the kings of England to alienate such territories from the crown, or to constitute a number of new governments, altogether independent of the sovereign legislative authority of the English empire, I can by no means concede to you." [2]

The governor then takes up Elizabeth's charter to

[1] Niles, *Principles and Acts of the Revolution,* pp. 80-81.
[2] Niles, *op. cit.,* p. 81.

Sir Walter Raleigh to which the Assembly had referred: "Now, if we could suppose the queen to have acquired, separate from her relation to her subjects, or in her natural capacity, which she could not do, a title to a country discovered by her subjects, and then to grant the same country to English subjects, in her public capacity as queen of England, still, by this grant, she annexed it to the crown. Thus, by not distinguishing between the crown of England and the kings and queens of England, in their personal or natural capacities, you have been led into a fundamental error, which must prove fatal to your system." [1]

"I am at a loss to know," he goes on, "what your ideas could be, when you say that, if the plantations are not part of the realm, they are not part of the kingdom, seeing the two words can properly convey but one idea. . . . I do not charge you with any design; but the equivocal use of the word realm, in several parts of your answer, makes them perplexed and obscure. Sometimes you must intend the whole dominion, which is subject to the authority of parliament; sometimes only strictly the territorial realm, to which other dominions are, or may be annexed. If you mean that no countries, but the ancient territorial realm, can, constitutionally be subject to the

[1] *Ibid.*

supreme authority of England, which you have very incautiously said is a rule of the common law of England—this is a doctrine which you will never be able to support. That the common law should be controlled and changed by statutes, every day's experience teaches; but that the common law prescribes limits to the extent of the legislative power, I believe has never been said upon any other occasion. That acts of parliaments for several hundred years past, have respected countries, which are not strictly within the realm, you might easily have discovered by the statute books. You will find acts for regulating the affairs of Ireland, though a separate and distinct kingdom. Wales and Calais, whilst they sent no representatives to parliament, were subject to the like regulations; so are Guernsey, Jersey, Alderney, &c. which send no members to this day. These countries are not more properly a part of the ancient realm, than the plantations, nor do I know they can more properly be said to be annexed to the realm, unless the declaring that acts of parliament shall extend to Wales, though not particularly named, shall make it so, which I conceive it does not, in the sense you intend.

"Thus, I think, I have made it appear that the plantations, though not strictly within the realm, have, from the beginning, been constitutionally subject to the supreme authority of the realm, and are so far annexed it, as to be, with the realm and the other dependencies upon it, one entire dominion; and that the plantation, or colony of Massachusetts-Bay in particular, is holden as feudatory of the imperial crown of England. Deem it to be no part of the realm, it is immaterial; for, to use the words of a very great authority in a case, in some respects analogous, 'being feudatory, the conclusion necessarily follows, that it is under the government of the king's laws and the king's courts, in cases proper for them to interpose, (like counties Palatine) it has peculiar laws and customs, *jura regalia,* and complete jurisdiction at home." [1]

In illustration of this view, he then proceeds to the acceptance of William and Mary in the colonies and the constitutional results supposed to follow: "Upon the revolution, the force of an act of parliament was evident, in a case of as great importance as any which could happen to the colony. King William and queen Mary were proclaimed in the colony, king and queen of England, France, and Ireland, and the dominions thereunto belonging, in the room of king James; and

---

[1] Niles, *Principles and Acts,* pp. 83-84.

this, not by virtue of an act of the colony, for no such act ever passed, but by force of an act of parliament, which altered the succession to the crown, and for which the people waited several weeks, with anxious concern. . . . If you should disown that authority, which has power even to change the succession to the crown, are you in no danger of denying the authority of our most gracious sovereign, which I am sure none of you can have in your thoughts. . . . By an act of parliament, passed in the first year of king William and queen Mary, a form of oaths was established, to be taken by those princes, and by all succeeding kings and queens of England, at their coronation; the first of which is, that they will govern the people of the kingdom, and the dominions thereunto belonging, according to the statutes in parliament agreed on, and the laws and customs of the same. When the colony directed their agents to make their humble application to king William, to grant the second charter, they could have no other pretence than, as they were inhabitants of part of the dominions of England; and they also knew the oath the king had taken, to govern them according to the statutes in parliament. Surely, then, at the time of this charter, also, it was the sense of our predecessors, as well as of the king and of the nation, that there was, and would remain, a supremacy in the parliament." [1]

He follows by citing the act of Anne continuing officers in their offices for six months after the death of the king, and the continuance in office of Governor Dudley under it as proof of the acceptance in Massachusetts of the act and of the authority of parliament to make it, and asserts generally that "for more than seventy years together, the supremacy of parliament was acknowledged, without complaints of grievance," [2] and thus concludes: "We all profess to be loyal and dutiful subjects of the king of Great Britain. His Majesty considers the British empire as one entire dominion, subject to one legislative power; a due submission to which, is essential to the maintenance of the rights, liberties, and privileges of the several parts of this dominion." [3]

A clearer exposition of the essential position of the English government could hardly be asked for, and the answer is equally clear and explicit. These two papers, in fact, the address of Hutchinson and the answer to it, are the best justification of the whole of my discussions that precedes them. To me they

---

[1] Niles, *Principles and Acts*, pp. 85-86.
[2] *Ibid.*, p. 86.
[3] *Ibid.*, p. 87.

seem a convincing demonstration of the enormous importance of the problem of the relation of realm and dominions and an incontrovertible proof that this importance was perfectly well understood at least by the keenest and most advanced of the American leaders—understood possibly better then than now. It will be necessary to quote at considerable length from the answer. Referring to the feudal basis of the king's power in the colonies, the assembly declare: "Upon the principles advanced, the lordship and dominion, like that of the lands in England, was in the king solely, and a right from thence accrued to him, of disposing such territories, under such tenure, and for such services to be performed, as the king or lord thought proper. But how the grantees became subjects of England, that is, the supreme authority of the parliament, your excellency has not explained to us. We conceive that, upon the feudal principles, all power is in the king; they afford us no idea of parliament."[1]

"Your excellency says, 'you can by no means concede to us that it is now, or was, when the plantations were first granted, the prerogative of the kings of England, to constitute a number of new governments,

---

[1] Niles, *Principles and Acts,* p. 88.

altogether independent of the sovereign authority of the English empire.' By the feudal principles, upon which you say 'all the grants which have been made of America are founded, the constitutions of the emperor have the force of law.' If our government be considered as merely feudatory, we are subject to the king's absolute will, and there is no authority of parliament, as the sovereign authority of the British empire. Upon these principles, what could hinder the king's constituting a number of independent governments in America? That King Charles the I did actually set up a government in this colony, conceding to it powers of making and executing laws, without any reservation to the English parliament, of authority to make future laws binding therein, is a fact which your excellency has not disproved, if you have denied it. Nor have you shown that the parliament or nation objected to it; from whence we have inferred that it was an acknowledged right. And we cannot conceive, why the king has not the same right to alienate and dispose of countries acquired by the discovery of his subjects, as he has to 'restore, upon a treaty of peace, countries which have been acquired in war,' carried on at the charge of the nation; or to 'sell and deliver up any part of his dominions to a foreign prince or state, against the general sense

of the nation;' which is 'an act of power,' or prerogative, which your excellency allows." [1]

"Your excellency says, that 'persons thus holding
under the crown of England, remain or become subjects of England,' by which, we suppose your excellency to mean, subject to the supreme authority of
parliament 'to all intents and purposes, as fully as
if any of the royal manors, etc., within the realm,
had been granted to them upon the like tenure.' We
apprehend, with submission, your excellency is mis-
taken in supposing that our allegiance is due to the
crown of England. Every man swears allegiance for
himself, to his own king, in his natural person. 'Every
subject is presumed by law to be sworn to the king,
which is to his natural person,' says Lord Coke—
Rep. on Calvin's Case. 'The allegiance is due to his
natural body;' and, he says, 'in the reign of Edward
II the Spencers, the father and the son, to cover the
treason hatched in their hearts, invented this damnable
and damned opinion, that homage and oath of allegiance was more by reason of the king's crown, that
is, of his politic capacity, than by reason of the person of the king; upon which opinion they inferred
execrable and detestable consequents.' The judges of

---

[1] Niles, *Principles and Acts,* pp. 88-89.

England, all but one, in the case of the union between
Scotland and England, declared that 'allegiance fol-
loweth the natural person, not the politic,' and, 'to
prove the allegiance to be tied to the body natural
of the king, and not to the body politic, the Lord Coke
cited the phrases of divers statutes, mentioning our
natural liege sovereign.' If, then, the homage and
allegiance is not to the body politic of the king, then
it is not to him as the head, or any part of that legislative authority, which your excellency says 'is equally
extensive with the authority of the crown throughout
every part of the dominion;' and your excellency's
observation thereupon must fail. The same judges
mention the allegiance of a subject to the kings of
England, who is out of the reach and extent of the
laws of England, which is perfectly reconcilable with
the principles of our ancestors, quoted before from your
excellency's history, but, upon your excellency's principles, appears to us to be absurdity. The judges,
speaking of a subject, say, 'although his birth was out
of the bounds of the kingdom of England, and out of
the reach and extent of the laws of England, yet, if
it were within the allegiance of the king of England,
etc., Normandy, Aquitain, Gascoign, and other places,
within the limits of France, and, consequently, out of
the realm or bounds of the kingdom of England, were

in subjection to the kings of England.' And the judges
say, *Rex et Regnum,* be not so relatives, as a king can
be king of but one kingdom, which clearly holdeth not,
but that his kingly power extending to divers nations
and kingdoms, all owe him equal subjection, and are
equally born to the benefit of his protection; and although he is to govern them by their distinct laws,
yet any one of the people coming into the other, is to
have the benefit of the laws, wheresoever he cometh.'
So they are not to be deemed aliens, as your excellency
in your speech supposes, in any of the dominions, all
which accords with the principles our ancestors held.
'And he is to bear the burden of taxes of the place
where he cometh, but living in one, or for his live-
lihood in one, he is not to be taxed in the other, because laws ordain taxes, impositions, and charges, as
a discipline of subjection, particularized to every particular nation.' Nothing, we think, can be more clear
to our purpose than the decision of judges, perhaps as
learned as ever adorned the English nation, or in
favour of America, in her present controversy with
the mother state.

"Your excellency says that, by 'our not distinguishing between the crown of England and the kings and
queens of England, in their personal or natural capacities, we have been led into a fundamental error.'

Upon this very distinction we have availed ourselves.
We have said, that our ancestors considered the land,
which they took possession of in America, as out of
the bounds of the kingdom of England, and out of
the reach and extent of the laws of England; and
that the king also, even in the act of granting the
charter, considered the territory as not within the
realm; that the king had an absolute right in himself
to dispose of the lands, and that this was not disputed by the nation; nor could the lands, on any solid
grounds, be claimed by the nation; and, therefore,
our ancestors received the lands, by grant, from the
king; and, at the same time, compacted with him, and
promised him homage and allegiance, not in his public
or politic, but natural capacity only.   If it be difficult for us to show how the king acquired a title to
this country in his natural capacity, or separate from
his relation to his subjects, which we confess, yet
we conceive it will be equally difficult for your excellency to show how the body politic and nation of
England acquired it." [1]

And so the assembly conclude that "the right of
being governed by laws, which were made by persons
in whose election they had a voice, they looked upon

---

[1] Niles, *Principles and Acts,* pp. 89-90.

as the foundation of English liberties. By the compact with the king, in the charter, they were to be as free in America as they would have been if they had remained within the realm; and, therefore, they freely asserted that they 'were to be governed by laws made by themselves, and by officers chosen by themselves.' " [1]

They answer the governor's argument based on the proclamation of William and Mary by pointing to the ability of the English to legislate for themselves in their Parliament by "the laws and customs of the same," i.e., by the *lex Parliamenti*, which guarantees representation. "According to this law, the king has an undoubted right to govern us. Your excellency, upon recollection, surely will not infer from hence, that it was the sense of our predecessors that there was to remain a supremacy in the English parliament, or a full power and authority to make laws binding upon us, in all cases whatever, in that parliament, where we cannot debate and deliberate upon the necessity or expediency of any law, and, consequently, without our consent; and, as it may probably happen, destructive of the first law of society, the good of the whole." [2]

---

[1] *Ibid.*, p. 91.
[2] Niles, *Principles and Acts*, p. 93.

And so they conclude, "We think your excellency has not proved, either that the colony is a part of the politic society of England, or that it has ever consented that the parliament of England or Great Britain, should make laws binding upon us, in all cases, whether made expressly to refer to us or not. . . . The question appears to us to be no other, than whether we are the subjects of absolute unlimited power, or of a free government, formed on the principles of the English constitution. If your excellency's doctrine be true, the people of this province hold their lands of the crown and people of England; and their lives, liberties, and properties, are at their disposal; and that, even by compact and their own consent, they were subject to the king, as the head *alterius populi* of another people, in whose legislature they have no voice or interest. . . . Is this the constitution which so charmed our ancestors, that, as your excellency has informed us, they kept a day of solemn thanksgiving to Almighty God when they received it?" [1]   Commentary would be superfluous.

---

[1] *Ibid.,* p. 94.

NOTE TO CHAPTER II

It is no part of my purpose to review the large and important contemporary American literature on the constitutional issues. It has been done more than once. The best bibliography of it remains the note of Justin Winsor in *Narrative and Critical History of America,* Vol. VI, pp. 68-112. Possibly the fullest contemporary discussions of the particular point taken up in this chapter—the constitutional relation of realm and dominions—is found in Daniel Leonard's papers, originally contributed to the *Massachusetts Gazette and Post-Boy,* over the name of *Massachusettensis* in 1774-5, and later published at Boston in collected form; together with the answers of John Adams writing as *Novanglus,* collected in his Works, edited by Charles Francis Adams, Boston, 1851, Vol. IV, pp. 1-177. See especially, *Massachusettensis* (Boston, 1775), pp. 41-42, 42-43, 45-46, 47, 51-52, 76 and 78. The author's fundamental argument was that "when a nation takes possession of a distant country, and settles there, that country though separated from the principal establishment or mother country, naturally becomes a part of the state" (p. 41). All the rest follows from this. "We are a part of the British empire are not aliens but natural-born subjects; and as such bound to obey the supreme power of the state, and entitled to protection from it" (p. 52). "Upon this point, whether the colonies are distinct states or not, our patriots have rashly tendered Great Britain an issue, against every principle of law and constitution, against reason and common prudence" (p. 76). John Adams's answer is the most elaborate exposition extant of the American interpretation of the constitutional problem of the empire, for which no summary or selection of extracts should be taken in lieu of the entire original. See especially, pp. 37, 38, 99-100, 105-106, 113, 114, 122, 123-125, 127, 133, 142-146, 151, 157-159, 162-163, 165, 169-172, 174, 176-177. At the end he sums up his conclusions as follows, with immediate reference to the grant of the Charter of Massachusetts Bay by Charles I and the inferences of *Massachusettensis* upon it: "But his acting as king of England 'necessarily supposes the territory granted to be a part of the English dominions, and holden of the crown of England.' Here is the word 'dominions' systematically introduced instead of the word 'realm.' There was no English dominions but the realm. And I say, that America was not any part of the English realm or dominions. And therefore, when the king granted it, he could not act as king of England, by the laws of England. As to the 'territory being holden of the crown, there is no such thing in nature or art.' Lands are holden according to the original notices of feuds, of the natural person of the lord. Holding lands in feudal language, means no more that the relation between lord and tenant. The reciprocal duties of these are all personal. Homage, fealty &c. and all other services, are personal to the lord; protection, &c. is personal to the tenant. And therefore no homage, fealty, or other services, can ever be rendered to the body politic, the political capacity, which is not corporated, but only a frame in the mind, an idea. No lands here, or in England, are held of the crown, meaning by it the political capacity; they are all held of the royal person, the natural person of the king. Holding lands, &c. of the crown, is an impropriety of expression; but it is often used; and when it is, it can have no other sensible meaning than this, that we hold lands of that person, whoever he is, who wears the crown; the law supposes he will be a right, natural heir of the present king forever." So, he concludes, when the grantees of the Massachusetts-Bay charter picked up the charter and migrated to America, "as soon as they arrived here, they got out

of the English realm, dominions, state, empire, call
it by what name you will, and out of the legal jurisdiction of parliament. The king might, by his writ
or proclamation, have commanded them to return; but
he did not" (pp. 176-177).

Among the most important of the other constitutional discussions about this time devoting some attention to the imperial problem, might be mentioned
James Wilson's *Considerations on the Nature and
Extent of the Legislative Authority of the British
Parliament,* 1774 (*Works of James Wilson, L.L.D.,*
edited by Bird Wilson, Esq., Philadelphia, 1804, vol.
III, pp. 199-246). Though much briefer than the
discussion of *Novanglus,* the fundamental position on
this question is the same. In the "advertisement" to
it, Wilson says he began his examination expecting to
find some line between those powers constitutionally
exercised by parliament in the colonies and those not,
but as a result of the examination he concluded that
no line really existed, and he ended by denying entirely the power of parliament in all matters whatsoever. Much the same is the conclusion of John
Dickinson's *Essay on the Constitutional Power of
Great Britain over the Colonies in America,* Philadelphia, 1774. (Reprint, Wilmington, Del., 1801.)
The author devotes some space to the justification of

the distinction between imperial matters and "matters of internal polity."

Mention should be made also of Jefferson's, *A Summary View of the Rights of British America, Set Forth in some Resolutions intended for the Inspection of the present Delegates of the People of Virginia, now in Convention,* 1774 (reprinted by Paul L. Ford, in *Writings of Jefferson,* I, p. 427). Of all the pamphlets setting forth the American contention at this time, Professor Channing considers this the "most worthy of analysis." (*A History of the United States,* Vol. III, p. 142.) He himself gives a résumé of its argument (*Ibid.,* pp. 142-145), and later admirably sums up its whole import in one phrase, when he says, "Imperial federation, not independency or democracy, was in Jefferson's mind." (*Ibid.,* p. 183.) "Imperial federation" is here used, of course, only in a generic sense.

There are many others, but in most the greater emphasis is placed upon natural law rather than upon the true constitution of the Empire. Some years before 1774, however, Thomas Pownall had thoroughly appreciated and carefully discussed the importance of this imperial problem, though he would have solved it in a way strikingly different. Even in the earlier editions of his famous *Administration of the Colonies,*

Pownall sees that the real problem lies in the relations of the realm and the dominions. His solution
is "that Great Britain may be no more considered
as the Kingdom of this Isle only, with many append-
ages of provinces, colonies, settlements, and other ex-
traneous parts, but as *A grand marine Dominion con-
sisting of our Possessions in the Atlantic and in
America united into a one empire, in a one center,
where the seat of government is.* (Fourth Edition,
London, 1768, pp. 9-10.)

He went far in the direction of Adams's later views
as to the actual relation of realm and dominions as
then existing, but this he regarded as dangerous to
liberty if left unchanged, because under it the king's
power over dependencies was entirely despotic. Hence
his proposed "Grand Marine Empire," virtually a new
imperial constitution on liberal principles.   In this
new empire he would insist, as the Long Parliament
did, that the people of England and of the dominions
alike should still be one "Commonwealth and Free
State."   But the government of this Commonwealth
he would no longer concede to "the supreme authority" of any parliament merely "of this Isle."   Instead he would extend it "through all the parts to
wheresoever the rights, interest or power of its dominions extend."   (*Ibid.,* p. 164.)

If Samuel and John Adams may be regarded as the earliest systematic expounders of the ideas of the recent school of colonial statesmen whose views are comprehended under the term "colonial nationalism," Thomas Pownall should as justly be considered the intellectual father of Lionel Curtis and the modern *Round Table* group of enlightened imperialists. (In this connection, Pownall's earlier proposals at Albany in 1754 and Franklin's plan of union are of some historical importance, but of course neither of these anticipated any but a strictly subordinate legislative body and one with very restricted purposes. On the other hand, some features of Galloway's plan, proposed in 1774, are undoubtedly drawn from this plan of 1754, and the plan is also significant in one respect, namely, that the acts of the Grand Council should be reviewable only by the King in Council in England. See, *New York Colonial Documents,* VI, pp. 889ff. I have ventured some comments on these transactions in *Wraxall's Abridgement of the New York Indian Records,* (*Harvard Historical Studies*) Introduction, pp. x-xl, xcvii ff.)

But following Pownall closely in order of time must come Joseph Galloway, on account of the plan he proposed to the Congress in 1774 as an alternative to Adams's principle of exemption from Parlia-

mentary authority. Some of the features of this plan
are a remarkable anticipation of the proposals of
recent imperialistic theorists, embodying as they do
Pownall's central idea of the oneness of the Empire,
but avoiding its chief defect, which arose from the
fact that under Pownall's scheme the Americans could
never have hoped to be more than an insignificant
minority in an English parliament, a practical objection that the Massachusetts Assembly had foreseen
and attempted to forestall by instructing its commissioners to the Congress on no account to consent to
it.   To obviate this practical difficulty, while at the
same time holding "in abhorrence the idea of being
considered independent communities on the British
government," Galloway proposed, "a British and
American legislature, for regulating" the general affairs of America "in which Great-Britain and the colonies, or any of them, the colonies in general, or more
than one colony, are in any manner concerned . . .
upon these principles of safety and freedom which are
essential in the constitution of all free governments,"
this legislature to consist of a President General appointed by the King, and a Grand Council of representatives of the people of the several colonies, the
said Governor and Council to "be an inferior and
distinct branch of the British legislature, united and

incorporated with it, for the aforesaid general purposes; and that any of the said general regulations
may originate and be formed and digested, either in
the Parliament of Great Britain, or in the said Grand
Council, and being prepared, transmitted to the other
for their approbation or dissent; and that the assent
of both shall be requisite to the validity of all such
general acts or statutes." (*Journals of the Continental Congress,* Ford, I, pp. 49-51; see also, pp. 43-
49.) Such a proposal, coming as early as 1774, ought
to place Galloway high on the roll among the most
liberal and enlightened British imperialists, but un-
fortunately for the plan itself, the Congress would
have none of it. They did in fact no longer "hold
in abhorrence the idea of being considered independent communities on the British government." Instead, they now adopted Adams's radical article four
and ordered that Galloway's plan be erased from
their minutes, "so that no vestige of it might appear
there." (See *Journals,* I, p. 51.)

For the earlier history of the growth of the views
set forth by John Adams in 1774, some statements
of Franklin, beginning at least as early as 1770 are
important. They are to be found in all editions of
Franklin's works. References to these and an interesting commentary upon them is to be found in Ber-

nard Holland's *Imperium et Libertas,* pp. 73-80. This whole book is valuable.

Even as early as 1766, Franklin in his celebrated examination by a committee of the House of Commons, had asserted that "the colonies are not supposed to be within the realm; they have assemblies of their own which are their parliaments, and they are, in that respect, in the same situation with Ireland" (*Parliamentary History,* Vol. XVI, col. 156), though his main argument was merely against internal taxation, and he admitted that as yet Americans went no further. When asked if this did not really imply a total denial of Parliament's binding authority, he answered significantly, "They never have hitherto. Many arguments have been lately used here to show them that there is no difference, and that if you have no right to tax them internally, you have none to tax them externally, or make any other law to bind them. At present they do not reason so, but in time they may be convinced by these arguments" (*Ibid.,* col. 158-159).

CHAPTER III

OF ALL the arguments urged by the Americans, one
alone supports the whole of their claim to a right of
exemption from parliamentary interference, the argument drawn from the constitutional relation of realm
and dominions.

It is too often forgotten that America claimed
nothing less than a *toto*[1] exemption as a matter of
constitutional right. Article four of the declaration
of the Continental Congress, quoted above, is the evident proof of that. But if true, but a moment's re-
flection will show, that no arguments drawn from
charters, or even from natural or fundamental law
will sufficiently justify it. Most colonies had no charters in 1774, and the existence of a fundamental law
as alleged put no limits to Parliament's authority,
beyond the very few matters established and guaranteed by the law of nature, or the fundamentals of
the English common law, or a combination of the two

in which natural law is "engrafted into the British constitution." All else is left wholly untouched.

So an opposition based on fundamental or natural law alone might properly be justified against *some* statutes of Parliament—the ones alone which infringed that law—but fundamental law provides no justification whatever for the total denial as made by the Congress of the whole legislative authority of Parliament over America. The only adequate justification for that lies in the argument drawn from the relation of realm and dominions, from a denial of the declaration of the Long Parliament in 1649 that the English Commonwealth is at once unitary and imperial. On that argument the Americans' cause must really stand or fall.

Possibly the proneness of American historians to deny the lawfulness of the Americans' claims in general may be due to a submergence of this fact: to an undue neglect of the imperial argument; and too exclusive an emphasis upon the less extensive justification furnished by fundamental law. For, on the basis of the latter argument alone, it is at once evident that in demanding a total exemption from parliamentary control, America was asking more than could be justified under her claims of right.

Neither is it altogether improbable that a like one-sided insistence on natural and fundamental law as the sole or main issue in the American struggle may sometimes have led to too complete an identification, especially by Whig historians, of the American contention with the contemporary opposition in England, particularly on the part of a wing of the Whig party, to the "King's friends" and their reactionary policies. The most liberal of the English statesmen did, it is true, accept the Americans' doctrines of natural law in part at least; but, so far as I can find, few indeed in England, outside a small knot of proscribed radicals,[1] would have been found in full and conscious agreement with the Adamses in 1774 upon the true constitution of the Empire.   Camden, Burke, Barré, and others were on fire against American taxation, and Pitt condemned it in unmeasured terms as without right, but it was Pitt who said, "Let the sovereign authority of this country over the colonies be asserted in as strong terms as can be assigned and be made to extend to every point of legislation whatsoever.

---

[1] Among others, Priestley; David Hartley the younger; Major John Cartwright, *American Independence the Glory and Interest of Great Britain,* 1774; Granville Sharp, in his *Declaration of the People's Natural Right to a Share in the Legislature,* 1774; and, possibly, most important, Dr. Richard Price, in *Observations on the Nature of Civil Liberty,* 1776, especially, Part I, Section III: *Of the Authority of one Country over another.* The argument of the last, however, is more political than constitutional.

That we may bind their trade, confine their manufactures, and exercise every power whatsoever, except that of taking their money out of their pockets without their own consent." "He did not rise above his generation to find the true science of colonial government."[1]

But though this claim under natural or fundamental law may be narrower than that furnished by the constitution of the Empire, it is yet important enough, especially in its influence on our later constitutional system, to warrant in an essay on the constitutional aspects of the American Revolution, some examination of the historical precedents upon which it was based and some attempt to estimate the correctness of the interpretation placed upon these so far as they go. To this, therefore, I must now turn, though briefly; and for greater clearness of treatment I shall try first to indicate the exact nature of the argument, exemplified by one ónly of the many statements of the "revolutionary" period, and then proceed to the earlier precedents for these in an attempt to estimate their merits; in which the distinction must be observed between (a) the law of nature as a legal justification, not merely political, (b) the "fundamentals" of the common law of England, and (c) a possible combi-

---

[1] G. B. Hertz, *The Old Colonial System,* p. 21.

nation of these two by which the law of nature is "engrafted into the British constitution."

The successive changes in American constitutional doctrine have been recently regarded as a continued "retreat." In fact, they show a steady development. In that development several stages are distinctly marked; first, a reliance on the charters, exemplified by Jeremiah Dummer's famous *Defence* of 1721. This stage definitely passed in 1765 when, after a considerable debate, the Stamp Act Congress determined to base their protests upon the wider rights of Englishmen; and charters thereafter played but a minor rôle as subsidiary to arguments of greater scope. The second constitutional stage was the general Whig argument that the English constitution, founded on natural law, was a free constitution, guaranteeing to all its subjects wherever they might be the fundamental rights incident to free government. The third and last constitutional phase of the controversy was the argument drawn from the constitution of the Empire as asserted in the declaration of the Congress of 1774. Then followed revolution and the final, political, non-constitutional appeal to natural law, no longer as a part of the British constitution, but as the rights of man in general; an appeal addressed no longer to Englishmen, but to the world.

In this constitutional treatment, it is only the first three of these that directly concern us. I have taken them up in an order the converse of the chronological, based on their relative importance; and in that order, the argument based upon natural and fundamental English law would seem to be second. This argument might be illustrated indefinitely by exponents both English and American, for on the basis of it the Americans and the most liberal of the Whigs in England were in exact agreement. The general argument is so well known that little definition is necessary and that little I shall take exclusively from James Otis's *Rights of the British Colonies,* published in 1764, one of the earliest and ablest pamphlets written from the natural law point of view. And its chief interest here lies in the fact that Otis's contention, though based on natural law, is nevertheless a constitutional one. Its entire validity depends on the correctness of its assumption that this law of nature is also a fundamental part of the English constitution. A slight examination, however, is enough to show that its starting point is the very antithesis of the final constitutional stand of America; for its whole argument is based on the central assumption that the Empire is *one* "Commonwealth and Free State," as the Long Parliament had said. Parliament's authority over that state is frankly accepted, and the subordinate character of the American assemblies fully conceded. But though the Empire is one and Parliament sovereign therein, it is a *free* state; and, as the Massachusetts Assembly said in 1768, "in all free states the constitution is fixed, and as the supreme legislative derives its power and authority from the constitution, it cannot overleap the bounds of it, without destroying its own foundation." [1]

As Otis put it, "There can be no prescription old enough to supersede the law of nature, and the grant of God Almighty; who has given to all men a natural right to be *free*." [2]

"The law of nature, was not of man's making, nor is it in his power to mend it, or alter its course." [3] Therefore, though Parliament has "an undoubted power and lawful authority" to bind the realm and the colonies alike, [4] even to the extent of annulling "every charter in America;" [5] every American is entitled to all the rights of an Englishman, independent of all charters, "by the law of God and nature,

---

[1] *Massachusetts Circular Letter,* Alden Bradford, *Speeches of the Governors of Massachusetts,* p. 134.

[2] *The Rights of the British Colonies,* pp. 16-17.

[3] *Ibid.,* p. 46.

[4] *Ibid.,* p. 49.

[5] *Ibid.,* p. 50.

by the common law, and by act of parliament,"[1] "from the British constitution which was re-established at the revolution."[2] But if Parliament through misinformation should wrongfully exercise its "uncontroulable" power in a colony, it must be obeyed. "They only can repeal their own acts,"[3] though if these are "against *natural* equity, the executive courts will adjudge such acts void."[4] But while all this is admitted, "To say the parliament is absolute and arbitrary, is a contradiction. The parliament cannot make 2 and 2 5: Omnipotency cannot do it. The supreme power in a state, is *jus dicere* only:— *jus dare,* strictly speaking, belongs alone to God. Parliaments are in all cases to *declare* what is for the good of the whole; but it is not the *declaration* of parliament that makes it so: There must be in every instance, a higher authority, *viz.* GOD. Should an act of parliament be against any of *his* natural laws, which are *immutably* true, *their* declaration would be contrary to eternal truth, equity and justice, and consequently void; and so it would be adjudged by the parliament itself, when convinced of their mistake."[5]

---

[1] *The Rights of the British Colonies,* p. 52.
[2] *Ibid.,* p. 56.
[3] *Ibid.,* p. 59.
[4] *Ibid.,* pp. 61-62.
[5] *Ibid.,* pp. 70-71.

In short, America's freedom consists for Otis in a
dependence upon a parliament which by definition must
be absolute but cannot be "arbitrary," and the most
despotic form of government imaginable would be a
freedom from Parliament and subjection to the king
alone.   This is Whig doctrine pure and simple, and
not more American than English.   Every line of it
was accepted by the liberal Whigs in England.   It is
not a distinctly colonial or American doctrine at all.

Hence in the Declaration and the three memorials
drawn up in the Stamp Act Congress, of which Otis
was a member, the stamp duties are objected to on
the purest Whig principles, and the constitutional position is the same as that expressed in *The Rights of
the British Colonies,* which appeared one year earlier.
The same is true of the *Massachusetts Circular Letter*
a few years later.   Massachusetts is still constitutionally English and Whig in 1768.   It is only claiming
with the full approval of many English statesmen "the
full enjoyment of the fundamental rules of the British constitution," and asserting with equal approval,
"that it is an essential, unalterable right, in nature,
engrafted into the British constitution, as a fundamental law, and ever held sacred and irrevocable by
the subjects within the realm, that what a man has
honestly acquired is absolutely his own; which he may

freely give, but cannot be taken from him without his consent."[1] No wonder Whig historians, like Sir George Otto Trevelyan have written sympathetically and even enthusiastically of an American opposition along such lines. The Americans were in truth fighting a battle for English liberty as well as American, and in England it was the same battle and for the time fought for the same principles. But 1768 was the high-water mark of Whiggism in America. There it stopped. From that time on the tide began to recede, and with it the sympathy of England. By 1774, America was no longer Whig. The doctrines of Camden had been exchanged for those of Molyneux, and by the next year the bulk of Englishmen, Whig and Tory alike, were united upon a policy of coercion.

Much as we are indebted to Whig principles—and the debt is very great—the Whig historians would make that debt even greater than it is. The Whigs have done much for England; they have not done all. Their doctrines did much for American freedom and constitutionalism; but they stopped short before the end was accomplished, and they stopped short because they had become inadequate.

The doctrine of the Whigs was really a doctrine of

[1] Alden Bradford, *Speeches of the Governors of Massachusetts,* p. 134.

the supremacy of Parliament.   By their creed the
British Empire was one commonwealth, and Parliament was its master.   Such a theory imposed no
checks on any abuses of Parliament's power; it was
sovereign and *legibus solutum*.   But the Americans
had come to doubt the correlative assertion of Whig
liberals that this irresistible power was never "arbitrary," that it could do no wrong.   And they were
now reaching the further conviction, through the repeated rejection of their remonstrances, that it firmly
intended to keep right on in a course which they considered a violation of their rights under the law of
nature and the fundamental law of England.   The
essential weakness of the Whig doctrine here clearly
appears.   It offered no more remedy against an oppressive parliament than the theory of divine right
had offered against a despotic king, and that was
only "sighs and tears."   Even the American Whig,
Otis, in his pamphlet admits that America's only re-
course is a petition to Parliament to repeal its objectionable acts, and the Stamp Act Congress asks for
no more.

No wonder there was a "retreat" from such a position after the enactment of the act suspending the
New York Assembly, the Boston Port Act, the Massachusetts Government Act, and the Administration of

Justice Act, all statutes, by the way, which have nothing directly to do with taxation.

Hence it came about that America's final constitutional position was not Whig at all: it was a position in some respects not merely non-Whig, but anti-Whig; for the doctrine of a parliament both omnipotent and imperial, against which they were really fighting, was more a Whig than a Tory principle. The traditional attitude of American historians toward both English and colonial history has been an overwhelmingly Whig one. From Whig sources, possibly on account of Puritan prejudices, their inspiration has almost wholly come, and the results have not been invariably fortunate.

So far then as America's final and fundamental constitutional demands as a part of the British Empire are concerned, our debt to England is slight, and rather to the Radicals than to the Whigs; and those Radicals were few and not influential. Our principal debt to Whiggism is really of quite another kind: it is found in those positive institutions of government whose foundations were laid long before the Revolutionary struggle. These were largely infused with Whig principles, and so they remained after the Revolution was over. These principles are still embodied in our present constitutional system, and to the same principles no doubt the actual revolution was in large part due, for no Whig could consistently deny a final "right of revolution"; but in the final and all-important stages of the constitutional struggle which preceded actual revolution, they played a very minor part. The Whigs brought on the English Revolution, but the American doctrine of 1774 was really a new revolt against one of the main principles of 1688. Even in 1839 it was an aristocratic radical who in defiance of Whig ministers published to the world the Magna Carta of the colonies, which embodies in practice if not in law the true American "revolutionary" principle.

If I am justified in distinguishing thus between the later and more important imperial theory and the fundamental-natural law theory which preceded, it is evident that the latter is far the less important of the two as a "cause" of the American Revolution. The overwhelming importance for American constitutional history of the theory of a fundamental law lies in its effect upon the positive constitutional doctrines which we think of as characteristically American, and as such I have treated its early history in another place.[1] But with that I am not now concerned, and since other-

---

[1] *The High Court of Parliament,* Chap. II.

wise both Whig principles and fundamental law are of minor importance, it hardly seems necessary to examine their beginnings with anything like the minuteness necessary for the imperial theory.

Arguments from natural law, however, it is worth remembering, played a far greater part generally in the eighteenth century than they do now, and while they were only a temporary phase of the American constitutional struggle, they were to return with redoubled force when revolution replaced constitutional opposition, and when the new construction in turn followed revolution. It is important, too, to bear in mind that the "natural" right to individual property on which the Whigs, following Harrington and Locke, laid so much stress, had played a great part in earlier contests with a doctrine of the divine right of kings which placed both subjects and their goods at the absolute disposal of their sovereign. The questionable way in which the same arguments have sometimes been used in our day to defend all vested interests and the deserved contempt into which they have fallen, largely in consequence, should not obscure their former services, or the fact that an appeal to them in the eighteenth century carried the greatest weight with intelligent and liberal minds.

So far as natural law concerns at all the constitutional struggle in America, its importance is due to the doctrine that it was "engrafted into the British constitution" as a part of English law.   So Lord Camden in 1766 denounced the Declaratory Act as a "Bill, the very existence of which is illegal, absolutely illegal, contrary to the fundamental laws of nature, contrary to the fundamental laws of this constitution, a constitution grounded on the eternal and immutable laws of nature." [1]

The three central points of this general argument are all included here, the law of nature, the fundamental law of the English constitution, and at least a partial identity of the two.

Each of these fundamental propositions had some earlier precedent in England to support it, and the first fell in with the views of the great philosophical jurists of the Continent in the eighteenth century; but the modern conception of sovereignty was fast encroaching upon them all, and the outcome was not affected by the fact that this was now the sovereignty of a representative assembly instead of a monarch. It is only one of the historical phases of the age-long antagonism between the ideas of law as truth and law as will.   The English, like the Romans and the canonists, had made a partial identification of the *jus*

---

[1] *Parliamentary History*, vol. 16, col. 178.

gentium and the *jus naturale,* and even of the *jus civile* and the *jus naturale.* For Coke the ancient customary law was also "the perfection of reason," and Saint German had said that the law of reason, a term the English lawyers preferred to the law of nature, was one of the chief grounds of English law. It is unnecessary here to enter upon these points.[1]

But the term law of nature has always been a vague one. Gaius and Ulpian and other contributors to the *Digest* were far apart on the question of its actual content, and it would be difficult indeed to include the Salic Law of France and the English law of succession in one "natural" system or to insist that so entirely English a thing as trial by jury was founded on the "immutable law of nature." In their first formal protest in 1765, the chief infringements of their rights under this law, of which the Americans complained, were two: "the invaluable rights of tax-

---

[1] For some discussion of these points and references to the sources, see James Bryce, *The Law of Nature,* in his *Studies in History and Jurisprudence,* vol. II, p. 556; Sir Frederick Pollock, *The Expansion of the Common Law,* pp. 107-138; *The History of the Law of Nature,* reprinted in his *Essays in the Law* (1922), pp. 31-79; Roscoe Pound, *The Spirit of the Common Law* (1921) ; *An Introduction to the Philosophy of Law* (1922) ; L. O. Pike, *Common Law and Conscience in the Ancient Court of Chancery,* (*Essays in Anglo-American Legal History,* vol. II, p. 722) ; Sir Paul Vinogradoff, *Reason and Conscience in Sixteenth Century Jurisprudence* (*Law Quarterly Review,* vol. 24, p. 373).

ing ourselves and trial by our peers."[1] By the second they meant, of course, trial by jury, and there is good ground for considering it a part of an English "fundamental law," though the "natural" basis of it is entirely lacking. Here they appealed solely to precedent, and the justice of their demand depends entirely on precedent, but precedent which is very strong.

On the side of taxation, their plea is still more important historically, because it constituted the first issue in the constitutional struggle. Important, however, as it is for this reason, it is only a part of the general argument from natural or fundamental law, and that whole argument itself was only a temporary phase in the developing constitutional views of the Americans. But, though the question of taxation was not the chief constitutional "cause" of the American Revolution, it has often been assumed to have been by historians of this period, and more has been written upon it, from 1765 up to the present, than upon any other constitutional issue in the conflict.

The abundance of this literature absolves me of the necessity of treating it again here, except in the most general way.

On the basis of natural law alone, a much better

---

[1] *Declaration of the Stamp Act Congress,* Niles, *Principles and Acts of the Revolution,* p. 165.

case could be made in 1765, for private property and consent to taxation than for trial by jury. Such a claim, of course, is exceedingly shaky, both philosophically and historically;[1] but these modern doubts of its validity would have been entertained by very few persons of any party in England or America between 1765 and 1776, and the force of the argument ought to be judged by us not alone by our own standards, but in the light of the prevalent social philosophy of the eighteenth century, particularly in England.

The English Revolution was the work of an aristocracy, and a landed aristocracy; its result, therefore, was a strengthening of the landed classes and its philosophy included a doctrine of the "natural" character of private property. None but the Jacobite remnant could continue to hold that all property was in the king and there were no communists observable. Locke insists on nothing more strongly than on the rights of individuals by the law of nature to what they have acquired, and this part of Locke's theory

---

[1] See *Property, its Duties and Rights,* London, 1915, a series of essays by various writers; Sir F. Pollock, Locke's Theory of the State (*Essays in the Law,* pp. 80-199); Carlyle, *A History of Mediæval Political Theory in the West,* vol. I, chap. 4, 12; vol. II, part I, chap. 5, part II, chap. 6; Roscoe Pound, *An Introduction to the Philosophy of Law,* chap. 5.

met with practically universal acceptance. No Whig, liberal or illiberal—and there were both—could repudiate this doctrine, and none did; and the great majority of the Tories were in full agreement with it by 1765. As a result of this unanimity on the ground of natural law, insistence on a right of parliamentary taxation of America came to turn almost exclusively on fact, the historical fact of the existence or non-existence of past cases of the levying of taxes by Parliament in territories beyond the realm, without first obtaining their consent directly, or through their representatives; and the question whether Englishmen within the realm then were or in past times ever had been held to be constructively in Parliament and therefore concluded by its impositions, when in fact they had no active part or voice in the election of any member. These two questions, the linking of taxation with representation, and the legal adequacy of "virtual representation," were the pivots on which this part of the controversy really turned. Hence though Camden might declare that "taxation and representation are inseparably united; God hath joined them, no British parliament can separate them;"[1] probably the arguments drawn from Ireland,

---

[1] *Parliamentary History,* vol. 16, col. 178.

Wales, the Channel Islands, Chester, Calais, or the history of Convocation, had greater influence. Certainly they seem to us to be more to the point.

They were not all decisive either way, as is the usual case in the citation of things long past as con-clusive justification for things now present; but some were more so than others. The fact that Chester was taxed, but received representation as a result of her objection to it, could be used by either side, according as emphasis was put on the previous taxation or on the resistance and subsequent representation. But Ireland, the Isle of Man, and the Channel Islands were stronger precedents for the American claim, both because they had never been taxed, and because they, like the plantations, were dominions geographically distinct from the realm, permanently separate from it, and never destined to become wholly absorbed in the same general parliamentary system which included all the English counties. The precedent of clerical taxation, too, was one that the opponents of America never faced quite openly. But all these instances, which are rehearsed without end in numberless pamphlets, in several important legal opinions, and in most modern books, will mean less if taxation was not the ultimate constitutional issue of the Revolutionary period. Only one phase of the taxation argument, significant on account of its bearing on the importance of consent, seems perhaps to have been somewhat slighted in the modern discussion of this subject, namely, the evidence furnished by recent investigation of the feudal origins and actual beginnings of parliamentary grants on a national scale in England.[1]

The argument of "virtual representation" as a justification for parliamentary taxation of the colonies proceeds on the assumption that Englishmen outside the realm are entitled to the rights of Englishmen within, but to no more, and that there are in fact in some parts of the realm itself many who are subject to Parliament's control, who exercise no direct voice whatever in the choice of members of that body; in short, that there are parts of England whose inhabitants neither in fact nor by right can choose members of the legislative body which of right levies taxes upon them. Since, therefore, colonial Englishmen are entitled to no more than Englishmen at home, no Americans whatever are entitled to more than the least privileged of those in England. The mere statement of such a principle shows its political injustice, especially when it is remembered how vast the in-

---

[1] See S. K. Mitchell, *Studies in Taxation under John and Henry III*, New Haven, 1914.

equalities of representation actually were in England at that time. But we are immediately concerned not with political justice or expediency, but only with the legal validity of the theory of virtual representation as a justification for parliamentary taxation of the colonies in the eighteenth century. And this legal validity depends in large measure on the correctness of the assumption that before the American Revolution there were parts of the realm of England itself that had in fact no actual representation whatever in the English Parliament, an assumption whose correctness, I believe to be open to very considerable doubt. The well-known cases of Manchester, Leeds, Birmingham, and other large places, often were and still are cited in proof of this theory; and it was notorious that these great towns sent no members to Westminster. But the argument based on them, insofar as it was a merely legal one—and beyond the law there was no argument whatever—seems to make a fatal confusion of under-representation and non-representation. Terribly under-represented as these great centres undoubtedly were, their representation, however small and inadequate, if they had any at all, was an actual and not a "virtual" one. It was legally entirely different from what America as a whole was expected to be satisfied with, which was no representation at all:

the true meaning of "virtual." And as a matter of
fact, these towns did have actual representation. The
pitiful smallness of it is a matter important politically,
but of no consequence in the legal argument. They
had what no American community possessed, for
every one of them lay in the body of some English
county, and the qualified townsmen could vote in the
county for the county members on a basis of entire
equality with all the rest of the electors of the county.
This might be inadequate, but it was actual. Lord
Mansfield's argument was in somewhat different form.
He chose to compare the lack of representation of
the American provinces to the absence of any special
representation in England for the Bank, the East India
Company, and other incorporated bodies; which of
course passed over in silence the fact that individuals
composing these corporations in England possessed
a parliamentary franchise which no American in any
colony enjoyed. The whole theory of virtual representation was as empty in law as it was unjust in
policy. Of all the arguments urged in England against
the American claims it was the least weighty; weak
in law, unsupported by fact, and sophistical even had
it been valid.

There remains the last, which in point of time was
the first, of the grounds of American opposition;

namely, the provisions contained in the various charters granted by kings of England to the colonists. This subject is of only minor importance among the causes of the Revolution. Like fundamental law, charters contributed more to our positive institutions of government than to the struggle resulting in our independence.

In the beginning, royal charters were regarded as transactions involving none but the king and the immediate grantee or those deriving their rights from the latter, and even the grantees themselves had no protection against the royal grantor's possible breach of his engagements. Concerning these, says Bracton in the thirteenth century, "neither justiciars nor private persons can or should dispute, and even should an ambiguity appear in them they cannot explain it. Even in doubtful and obscure matters or where some phrase has a double meaning the will and interpretation of the lord king must be awaited, since it is his to interpret to whom belongs the right to establish" '(*cum eius sit interpretari cuius est condere*).[1] Then follows the famous puzzling *addicio* in which the king

---

[1] Bracton, folio 34 b (in Professor Woodbine's edition, vol. II, p. 109). This may be a reminiscence of *Digest*, 50, 17, 96, (*De Diversis Regulis*), where Marcianus says, *"In ambiguis orationibus maxime sententia spectanda est eius, qui eas protulisset."*

is said to have a superior in God, in the law, and in his curia, "namely the earls and barons, since earls (comites) are so called from being as it were associates (socii) of the king and he who has an associate has a master."[1]   And it is said that "no one can interpret the act or the charter of the king so as to render the king's act or charter null;" probably, as Maitland surmises, a prohibition of dispensations through a *non obstante*.   The second of these inconsistent passages was probably no part of Bracton's original text, though it was written before the thirteenth century was out.

Clearly, views were divided at that time as to the nature and extent of the "prerogative," but it is evident that the holder of a charter from the king was in a position none too secure.   It is no doubt true, as Dr. Ehrlich has said, that kings seldom or never broke their charters "without justification"; but at first the justifications were many, and as a matter of fact "Kings often broke their charters," and frequently had to be paid not to break them.[2]   As time went on,

---

[1] On this *addicio*, see Woodbine, *Bracton*, vol. I, pp. 252, 332; Maitland, *Bracton's Note Book*, vol. I, pp. 29-33; G. B. Adams, *The Origin of the English Constitution*, p. 309; McIlwain, *High Court of Parliament*, p. 101; Ludwik Ehrlich, *Proceedings against the Crown*, (*Oxford Studies in Social and Legal History*, vol VI, p. 50 (1921).

[2] Ehrlich, *Proceedings against the Crown*, p. 10.

however, "the common profit of the Realm" came in practice to be more and more regarded,[1] and this meant that in actual fact the provisions of a charter granted by the king came ultimately to be enforced almost as effectively as a matter of grace as those granted by another subject would have been through the regular procedure.[2] But theory was later to play a large part in the history of American charters, and through all these practical changes the theory remained for centuries unchanged. So Stanford wrote in 1590, "Petition is all the remedie the subject hath when the king seiseth his land, or taketh away his goodes from him, hauing no title by order of his lawes so to do, in which case the subiect for his remedie is driuen to sue unto his Soueraigne Lord by way of Petition onely; for other remedie hath he not. . . . And therefore is his petition called a petition of right, because of the right the subiect hath against the king by the order of his Lawes, to the thing he sueth for. And thys petition may be sued.as well in the Parliament as out of the Parliament, and if it bee sued in the Parliament, then it may be enacted and passe as an act of parliament, or els to be ordered in

---

[1] *Ibid.*, p. 146.
[2] Dr. Ehrlich gives the best account of this development.

like manner as a petition that is sued out of the parliament." [1]

It seems clear that up to the end of Elizabeth's reign a royal grant or charter made by the king by prerogative "in right of his Crown," remained "a branch of the king's prerogative in the hands. of a subject," and that the property, powers, and immunities thus conveyed by a king were subject only to such limits as affected the prerogative itself. It is also clear that if the exercise of such a power infringed the right of another subject under the law of the land and a remedy lay against the crown, it was not by action as of right, but by petition of right as a matter of grace. Such petitions could be heard and determined not by the lower courts alone, but by the High Court of Parliament as well, but in either case the decision would be strictly a judicial procedure according to the *lex terrae* and neither by the *Lex Parliamenti* nor merely *per arbitrium,* though its form might possibly be either by petition or by act of Parliament. If, however, a king's grant lay "above the course of the common law," or even "out of the ordinary course of the common law," it might be argued, and I think it was then generally held, that there was no remedy

---

[1] *An Exposition of the Kinges Praerogative,* folio 72

but of royal grace. Apparently, the beginning of parliamentary encroachment on this, "the choicest flower"
of the prerogative, is to be dated from the great debates in Parliament on monopolies in 1601, "when such
charters of incorporation were first taken notice of." [1]
In these debates Bacon objected to proceeding by bill.
"The Use," he declared, "hath been ever, by Petition
to Humble our selves to Her *Majesty,* and by Petition to desire to have our Grievances redressed. . . .
I say, and I say again, That we ought not to deal or
meddle with, or judge of Her *Majesty's* Prerogative.
I wish every Man therefore, to be careful in this
Point." [2] Later he said, "The Bill is very injurious,
and ridiculous: Injurious, in that it taketh, or rather
sweepeth away her Majesties Prerogative; and Ridiculous, in that there is a Proviso, That this Statute
shall not extend to Grants made to Corporations
[municipal corporations and gilds probably.] That is
a gull to sweeten the Bill withall, it is only to make
Fools Fond. All men of the Law know, that a Bill

---

[1] Argument of Sir George Treby, afterward Lord Chief Justice,
in the Great Case of Monopolies, *East India Company* v. *Sandys*
(1683-1685), *Howell's State Trials,* X. col. 385. In the same case
Holt, afterward Chief Justice, said: "In the 43rd of the queen,
the discourse of Monopolies first began in parliament." *Ibid.,*
col. 381.

[2] *Heywood Townshend's Historical Collections* (1680), p. 232.

which is only Expository to Expound the Common-Law, doth Enact nothing, neither is any *Proviso* good therein. . . . Therefore I think the Bill unfit, and our proceedings to be by Petition."[1] For the time the impassioned warning of Secretary Cecil and the effusive promises of the Queen herself postponed the threatened action, but the continuance of the abuses of monopolies and the growing realization by Parliament of its legislative powers renewed the struggle with added bitterness in the reign of her successor. The subject was revived in 1614, and in James's last Parliament the blow finally fell in the Statute of Monopolies, an *Act Concerning Monopolies and Dispensations of Penal Laws, and the Forfeitures thereof*.[2] It declared that all monopolies existent or in future to be granted within England and Wales were, "altogether contrary to the Laws of this Realm, and so are and shall be utterly void and of none effect," and, what is more significant still, asserted the principle that "all such Commisions, Grants, Licenses, Charters, Letters Patents, Proclamations, Inhibitions, Restraints, Warrants of Assistance," etc., "ought to be and shall be for ever hereafter examined, heard, tried and determined by and according to the Common

---

[1] *Heywood Townshend's Historical Collections,* p. 238.
[2] 21 James I, chap. III (1624).

Laws of this Realm, and not otherwise." Among the exceptions to the operation of the act were municipal and gild charters, but only "within this Realm." For the realm it was probably the most salutary and telling blow thus far ever struck at the king's prerogative, but it was also a precedent of the most menacing kind for the future action of Parliament against colonial charters and against the security of the tenure by which the Americans enjoyed the liberal concessions contained in them.

The American charters themselves, however, did not come within the operation of the Statute of Monopolies. The real importance of the statute therefore is that a beginning had been made of Parliament's encroachment upon the prerogative, which in time was to swell into an unchecked power to sweep away all barriers to Parliament's action contained in any grant from any king. For the time the greatest danger to charter rights still lay in the prerogative itself, or in judicial process against colonies where there had been an actual or apparent abuse of charter powers, as in Massachusetts. In the same year as the passage of the act against monopolies, *quo warranto* proceedings were instituted against the Virginia charter, which resulted in a judgment against it.[1] Mean-

---

[1] For an account of this and the interesting attempt of the

178 THE AMERICAN REVOLUTION

while the menace of Parliament was only beginning, so far as charters were concerned, but the Statute of Monopolies was ominous.

In fact charters were exposed to attack from no less than three separate quarters, the prerogative, the courts, and the Parliament. Judges' patents were among those expressly excepted from the Statute of Monopolies, and in 1628 Charles I unsuccessfully tried to force Sir John Walter, Chief Baron of the Exchequer to surrender his patent, though his tenure was *quamdiu se bene gesserit*. On Walter's refusal, Charles did not venture to institute judicial proceedings or to withhold from him his salary and fees; but he was able to command Walter to refrain from acting as a judge, and the command was obeyed.[1] Charles II succeeded in doing the same thing in the case of Justice Archer.[2] Plainly, on such precedents, patents and charters not within the Statute of Monopolies were exposed to considerable danger from the prerogative alone, and the colonies felt the full brunt

members of the Virginia Company to get their case into the House of Commons, see H. L. Osgood, *The American Colonies in the Seventeenth Century,* III, pp, 47-53.

[1] *American Political Science Review,* vol. VII, No. 2 (May, 1913), p. 221; *A Vindication of Mr. Fox's History of the Early Part of the Reign of James the Second,* by Samuel Heywood (London, 1811), Appendix No. 1.

[2] Heywood, *op. cit.*

of it in time. The English Revolution itself did not end this danger, for even in 1690 Lord Holt advised the President of the Council that the King might appoint a governor for Maryland in violation of Lord Baltimore's charter, without any judicial process whatever against the charter, provided only that the governor must be responsible to Lord Baltimore for the profits. This was naked prerogative, and if Lord Baltimore was in bad case as a result of it, how much worse the inhabitants of Maryland![1] Baltimore's original charter had provided for representative institutions and the rights of Englishmen, and now all guarantee for their continuance was swept away by this opinion, though they had been enjoyed for a generation and more. The fact that this charter was in fact as well as form a provincial constitution for some thousands of Englishmen affected its legal status not in the slightest degree. From that point of view the people of Maryland did not exist, but only the grantor and the grantee of the document, and even the grantee's legitimate claims were satisfied, if his rev-

---

[1] Forsyth, *Cases and Opinions on Constitutional Law*, p. 380. The editor ventures the opinion that this cannot be considered sound law. It is rather difficult to say why. It certainly was an extreme exercise of prerogative, especially after the Revolution, but exactly on what ground it could be legally impeached the editor does not disclose.

enues alone were secured to him.   Charters were a
rather slight protection against prerogative, and John
Adams might have found it out to his sorrow if independence had not come when it did.   Pownall's
fears had a real justification, and it is little wonder
that New York and South Carolina objected when
such a ground as charter rights was proposed in 1765
as the basis of their claims against the Stamp duties.

But the danger lay not in prerogative alone.   Charters, by a right that none could deny, might be vacated
by a writ of *scire facias* or *quo warranto* in cases of
abuse of the powers granted by charter or by acts
ultra vires.   No lawyer could deny this, and all Americans knew that some colonies had repeatedly committed such acts.   The loss of the first charter of
Massachusetts had thus occurred in 1684, and it would
be extremely difficult to prove the illegality of the
judgment against it.   The trouble was that the inevitable development of the colonies had in almost
all cases stretched the charter powers under which
they existed.   The lamentable fact was that the very
salutary growth of colonial institutions thus made
them undeniably illegal.   The charters had in fact
become free constitutions in America.   In law they
remained only mediæval grants, and in law there were
no parties to them but the grantor and grantee, though

they regulated the lives and relations of increasing thousands of subjects of the king.

The law was unquestioned, it cannot now be questioned, but the practical result was deplorable. In the time of Charles II and James II the successful attacks on the London charter and the Oxford colleges by judicial process, together with well-known cases nearer home, must have convinced Americans that their protection by charter was slender indeed; and especially in the reign of James II, when judicial tenure was weakest and judicial independence, as a result, the slightest, this danger was a very real one both in the realm and in the dominions.

That part of the Act of Settlement of 1701, which made judicial tenure more secure for England was never extended to America, hence it remained a grievance there to the very end, of which complaint was made repeatedly but in vain, that in the colonies judicial tenure still remained *quamdiu nobis placuerit*. On this side, as well as the side of mere prerogative, charters were only a broken reed.

But the newest danger was probably the greatest, the danger from Parliament itself. If Parliament could destroy a royal monopoly in the realm as was done in 1624, why not in the dominions?

After the English Revolution Parliament saw little

reason why their power in this respect should stop at the low-water line. The act of 1624 had not affected colonial charters, but that was merely because in 1624 there were no grievances in the colonies that Parliament cared to remove. That act, however, had fully established Parliament's authority, and the extent of its exercise was a matter wholly within its own discretion. It is difficult to see why this was not true. Bacon's original objection was very acute. If Parliament in 1601, in enacting such a provision could restrict its operation to certain classes of monopolies, either the exception of these was invalid, or the whole enactment was a real legislative encroachment upon prerogative and no mere exposition of common law. This was what made the matter a thing of such fundamental importance, for this act when it was passed was no mere expository act: it was a real act of sovereign power, which by direct legislation destroyed a most important branch of the royal prerogative. By 1689, all hesitation about the use of such a power by Parliament, so strong in 1601, had been completely swept away by the civil wars and the Revolution, and nothing but expediency stood in the way of the Parliament's extension of the precedent of 1624 to any part or to all parts of the ancient power which the king had in right of his crown. Prerogative was in fact no longer that power which the king had "above the ordinarie course of the common law."[1] It had already come to be no more than "the residue of discretionary or arbitrary authority, which at any given time is legally left in the hands of the Crown."[2] The Parliament had taken away some, it had an unlimited right to take away more, or, if need be, all. The very existence of such power has alone made its exercise rarely necessary.

Unlike the parliamentary pretensions of authority over the dominions as such, this was not all the result of revolution. The precedent for it in the Act of Monopolies had been duly enacted and had long been fully accepted, and that before the migration of the ancestors of the great majority of Americans now to be affected by it. This new danger to the colonies was not long held in abeyance after the Revolution. As early as 1701 a bill was introduced in Parliament for "Reuniting to the Crown the Governments of several Colonies and Plantations in America." The bill failed of passage, but attempts were made again in 1706 and 1715. Only chance and influence, or at

---

[1] Cowell's *Interpreter*, s.v. *Prerogative*, in the editions of 1607 and 1637. In subsequent editions the definition was altered.
[2] A. V. Dicey, *The Law of the Constitution*, seventh edition, p. 420.

most arguments from expediency, prevented the passage of these bills. It was no lack of assurance in the Parliament of the existence of such a power, nor any belief in its limits, which prevented their passage. The whole story has been admirably set forth by Miss Kellogg in her paper on the American Colonial Charter,[1] to which the reader is referred for a fuller account of this phase of the history of the charters.

By 1765 then, and long before, the colonists were fully aware of the constitutional weakness as well as the practical inadvisability of a reliance upon charters alone. When the question came up in the Stamp Act Congress, some of the delegates from colonies having favourable charters, proposed such a course, but the arguments of the less favoured colonies prevailed, and the liberal Whig doctrine of natural and fundamental law was substituted.[2]

The wisdom of this cannot be questioned. There is no doubt of the weakness of the charter claim, and Lord Mansfield's argument, so far as the strict law of royal grants is concerned, seems unanswerable—

---

[1] Louise Phelps Kellogg, *The American Colonial Charter* (Annual Report of the American Historical Association for 1903), vol. I, p. 185ff, especially chap. IV, *Parliamentary Proceedings against the Charters*, p. 278ff.

[2] Richard Frothingham, *The Rise of the Republic of the United States*, p. 188.

that the colonies such as Connecticut, Rhode Island, and Massachusetts were "all on the same footing as our great corporations in London." [1]

This was, as Professor Schlesinger says, unquestionably a "retreat" from a position that had never been tenable, but I doubt whether the position was ever really held by more than a handfull of thoughtful Americans after the issue was fairly joined between them and the mother country.

This ground of opposition was deliberately rejected at the outset in the Stamp Act Congress, after full consideration; and in 1768 this rejection was made more explicit in the claim of the *Massachusetts Circular Letter,* to the right to an exemption from parliamentary taxation "exclusive of any consideration of charter rights." [2]

The wisdom of this line of action was soon to be proved by Parliament's enactment of the Massachusetts Government Act and the Administration of Justice Act, in which the provisions of the Massachusetts charter of 1691 then still in force were treated as non-existent.

---

[1] *Parliamentary History,* vol. 16, col. 175.
[2] Alden Bradford, *Speeches of the Governors of Massachusetts,* p. 134.

CHAPTER IV

CONCLUSION

IF THE opposition to Parliament of some of the leading American statesmen just before the American Revolution is not to be called in large part a constitutional opposition, one of three other explanations of their actions would seem the only reasonable alternative: they were either trying to throw off an actual economic burden, crushing in its weight and oppressive in its character, or the rights which they professed to be asserting were only the creation of heated imaginations or uninstructed minds; or, if neither of these views be tenable, they were from the beginning merely cloaking under a specious claim of constitutional right in which they did not really believe, a settled determination to be absolutely independent of Great Britain.

The "economic historians" themselves have performed a valuable service in dispelling the first of these views. We are no longer hypnotized by Bancroft's eloquence into believing that all Americans were

ipso facto patriots and all Englishmen oppressors
per se. The burdens actually imposed by the British
Parliament were very light indeed. The stamp tax
had been withdrawn almost as soon as imposed when
the surprised Parliament found what an opposition it
aroused in America. The taxes that succeeded it were
utterly insignificant in amount, and of the least irri-
tating kind known to tax gatherers. The Americans
knew they should pay their fair share of the costly
Seven Years' War, and they knew that they had not
all done so. It is difficult to characterize this as in-
tolerable oppression, and all American historians—all
at least who claim descent from the revolutionists
themselves—have long ceased to do so. The American colonists in 1774 or 1775 stood no greater risk
of actual impoverishment by taxation than Hampden
did when he refused payment of Ship Money. The
fact is that Ship Money was neither burdensome in
amount nor unreasonable in character. Englishmen
of every county today pay many times its amount for
the very same purpose. But Hampden is called neither
a knave nor a fool for refusing to pay a sum he never
would have missed, for a purpose of which he probably entirely approved. He opposed Ship Money because he considered it to be without warrant of law:
his objection was constitutional. True he was afraid

of the ultimate political consequences: he feared that the king would thus eventually be enabled to subsist without a dependence on Parliament. But the immediate and only colourable ground of his objection was illegality, lack of precedent. So the Americans were many of them honestly convinced of the existence in Parliament of a settled design to "enslave" them. It would be idle to deny that fears for the future affected their attitude. They and Hampden, like Becket in the twelfth century and the barons of Henry III in the thirteenth, were above all afraid lest their acts in sufference of unprecedented claims *traherentur in consequentiam,*[1] *unde posteri gravarentur,*[2] and history as a whole vindicates the reasonableness of their fear. But the immediate object of their attack was the "unconstitutionality," the unprecedented character of Parliament's present claim to authority over them, and the cases of its exercise which had already occurred.

It is difficult indeed to say that such an opposition on the part of men like James Wilson and John Adams could have been the result of ignorance or stupidity. If their claim was "absurd," however, as it seems the

[1] Matthew Paris, *Chronica Majora* (Rolls Series), vol. IV, p. 186 (1242).

[2] Edward Grim, Life of St. Thomas of Canterbury, in *Materials for the History of Thomas Becket* (Rolls Series), vol. II, p. 374.

fashion now to call it, it is hard to acquit them of such a charge or of one much worse. In fact their opposition was not absurd, and neither groundless nor insincere. Hampden was not oppressed, and neither were they. But both Hampden and they were sincerely convinced that their legal rights were being infringed and that a sufferance of it must have the most disastrous consequences. Hampden's justification is Adams's. If we admit the one it will be hard to deny the other. An English court decided against Hampden's claim, as Parliament declared against Adams's; and some study of the Case of Ship Money and its background has led me to think that the precedents on the side of the king's judges in the former case were, to say the least, no less conclusive than those on which Parliament relied in 1774.[1] It will hardly do to dismiss the reasoned arguments of Wilson and Adams as "absurd," or to imply, as one must in such a case, that they were either hopelessly befogged or deliberately insincere. Some historians seem almost to have preferred the latter explanation. The late Professor Goldwin Smith wrote some very interesting pages recounting the dissolute and untutored youth of Patrick Henry and the earlier financial

---

[1] McIlwain, *The High Court of Parliament,* pp. 149-150, 301-304.

failures of Samuel Adams, and no doubt much of this is true. But the inference the author would have us draw from it is neither a just nor a necessary one. In the revolutionary struggle these men were no mere irresponsible and idle adventurers secretly scheming from the first to overthrow British authority, if not for their own individual advantage, at least on an insincere pretext of redressing constitutional wrongs. There is suspiciously much in these histories of the earlier career of Patrick Henry and Samuel Adams. Not so much is said of the training of John Adams and of James Wilson. As a whole, this radical group were certainly not ignorant; in the foregoing essay I have set forth some precedents which seem to me to make it unnecessary to assume that they were insincere. But they were a minority of the colonists, it is said, and this is probably strictly true, till after the Declaration of Independence at least, or the appearance of Paine's *Common Sense*.[1]

From 1774 to the latter part of 1775 at least, the leaders of the Congress probably held more advanced and radical constitutional ground than the majority of Americans interested at all in constitutional matters; but it was still a constitutional ground. On May

---

[1] *Common Sense* was published on January 10, 1776, M. D. Conway, *The Life of Thomas Paine,* vol. I, p. 61.

26, 1775, Lord North's concessions were reported to
them. On July 31 these were rejected as "insidious,"
because Parliament had not renounced its right "to
alter our charters and establish laws, and leave us
without any security for our lives or liberties." [1]

Nothing less than a renunciation of all authority in
internal matters at least could have satisfied the Congress's claims after 1774; and, far as they went, these
proposals of Lord North fell far short of that; besides
the Congress had been given to understand semi-offi-
cially that "no further relaxation" could be admitted. [2]
The congressional leaders were in all probability in
advance of the bulk of the Americans up to this time,
but all radical movements begin with a few, and it
was not long before a current of popular sentiment
irresistible, even if not unanimous, forced the Congress far beyond the most radical constitutional position hitherto held by its leaders, and swept them on
to the revolutionary pronouncement of the fifteenth
of May, 1776. It is admirably recounted by Frothingham [3] in his tenth chapter and need not be repeated.
Thereafter, as the orthodox historians truly point out,
the congressional statesmen appeal no more to their

---

[1] *Journals of the Continental Congress*, II, 232.
[2] *Ibid.*, p. 72.
[3] *The Rise of the Republic of the United States.*

rights as Englishmen. They have perforce become revolutionaries and are no longer constitutionalists. Their many constitutional appeals have fallen upon deaf ears. They turn now to another audience and with another appeal. The Declaration of Independence is a totally different kind of document from any of its predecessors. For the first time the grievances it voices are grievances against the King, and not against Parliament. It is addressed to the world, not to Great Britain, and naturally the ground of such a protest will be one understood by a world that knows little of the British constitution and cares less: it will be based on the law of nature instead of the constitution of the British Empire. And this is what a recent historian calls a "retreat from one strategic position to another." When their appeal to their rights as Englishmen "became untenable, they invoked the doctrines of the rights of man." [1]

Because the Congress in the end appealed to the world on the only ground to which eighteenth century continental Europe would have listened, and relied on the only principles understood by them, or for which they cared: because this first revolutionary appeal of America is based on political theory instead

[1] *New Viewpoints in American History,* Schlesinger, p. 179.

of constitutional law; the assumption is made that this change could only be the result of the "untenable" character of the earlier constitutional position. *Non sequitur.*

The American opposition loses its constitutional character in 1776 and becomes a subject no longer susceptible of constitutional treatment. It is therefore, only with this "untenable" constitutional position from which the Americans finally "retreated" into revolution that we are immediately concerned.

It has been the purpose of this essay to attempt to make clear exactly what this constitutional position was and what it was not, and to estimate the validity of the construction of earlier constitutional precedents on which it was based.

In conclusion, then, it is submitted, that there was a *bona fide* constitutional issue which preceded the American Revolution, and from which it in part resulted, an issue which was by no means a mere pretext, sincere or otherwise, for a demand for the removal of burdens, whether lawful or unlawful, of a quite different kind.

In this indictment which the Americans brought against the British Parliament there are several counts, an infringement of the colonial charters, a violation of the law of nature, which is a part of English law, and a breach of the constitution of the British Empire.   Of these counts, the last is the essential one, and the most far-reaching, in which the other lesser demands are included or to which they are wholly subsidiary, and the only one of the three which offers a complete justification for the whole of the American demands.   The alleged inability of Parliament to legislate in any matter for any colony of course precludes all parliamentary taxation.   It leaves the royal prerogative as the only imperial authority over the dominions acknowledged as legal, and charters are merely the pacts between the King and his dominions by which he has engaged that this prerogative will not be abused.

Thus in their demand that the alleged unconstitutional control of Parliament should cease, the Americans faced the alternative of a royal prerogative with no limits to its power except the self-limitation imposed by the promises made by Kings to the colonists in their charters, a limitation which had proved to be of very doubtful value.   This was the weak spot in the American position and it was pointed out by enemies in Parliament and by such a friend as Thomas Pownall.   Pownall was sincerely fearful of the establishment of a despotic authority through the prerogative, and it is impossible to say that his fear was

groundless. It was a real danger, and one not wholly
obviated before the full acceptance of the principles
of Wakefield, Buller, and Lord Durham. But in 1774
the Americans were engaged primarily with Parliament. They had abandoned the central principle of
Whiggism, and were now persuaded rightly or
wrongly that the immediate danger to their liberties
lay in Parliament itself. The "unconstitutional" acts
which roused their ire were acts of Parliament, and
in view of the history of Irish relations, it is hard
to call entirely unreasonable either their sentiments
or their presentiments. Nor should the fact of George
III's known antipathy to America affect our judgment
in this case, for the danger to be expected from the
King in 1774 must have appeared to a close observer
of affairs in England at that time to be due far more
to his "influence" than to his prerogative, and it is
impossible to say that such an impression was unjus-
tified. For the time at least the Americans left out
of consideration all constitutional dangers but the present one of Parliament and acknowledged as the alternative a prerogative hampered by no barriers but the
uncertain promises contained in their charters. In
so doing they undeniably incurred enormous risk of
future oppression through a prerogative unchecked by
Parliament, as their Whig opponents were not slow

in pointing out. But Whiggism had already failed as a theory of Empire, and American independence soon afterward put an end to prerogative as well, so one can only guess what might have followed. Later, in the new British Empire, under conditions more favourable, a satisfactory solution was at last found, and, as usual in such cases, a solution somewhat different from the one anticipated by any of the original antagonists on either side. But what would have immediately followed in 1774 had England accepted America's terms, none can say.

The general considerations just set forth led me to treat the imperial question as the central issue of the American struggle, and to pass over matters of fundamental law, taxation, or charters more rapidly, as of minor importance, or because they were included in and comprehended by the wider imperial question. On that question the rightfulness or wrongfulness of the American contention was, I think, really judged by the most acute of the statesmen of the revolutionary period. Upon it the relative merits of their claims must be estimated today. It is only fairness thus to estimate their claims by the strongest arguments they presented, rather than upon weaker or minor considerations. This, I submit, has not always been done, and to the detriment alike of the reputation of the revolu-

tionary statesmen and of the satisfactoriness of some
of the modern books.

Though the conclusions I have reached through an
examination of the precedents for the constitution
of the Empire are, as I believe, warranted by these
precedents; they are such as have been recently termed
"absurd" by one American historian, and thought so,
I suspect, by others. I do not, on that account, however, feel justified in retorting in kind, in good seventeenth century fashion, sorely as one might be tempted
to do so. The contention of the eighteenth century,
constitutionally considered, was the result of two vary-
ing and inconsistent interpretations of the same set of
precedents, and these precedents had been gradually
formed many of them centuries before the interpretations were made, under wholly different and quite un-
familiar conditions practical and intellectual. It was
this that made the later inconsistent interpretations
possible, and it is this that should now make one wary
of pronouncing too confidently that either of them
must of necessity be wrong or "absurd." He would
be a rash man who said that Lord Mansfield's constitutional theory was "absurd"; and worse, if he
inferred that Mansfield must have been insincere in
holding it. Had Calvin's Case not established the
English doctrine of the nature of allegiance, one might

hesitate long between the views of Bacon and Doddridge upon that important subject.   Neither view is
absurd, but Bacon's view had been received as law
before the Americans migrated.   The later divergence
of Adams and Mansfield is not unlike it, but it was
to be adjudicated only by the sword.   It is not entirely
easy to say with absolute assurance that the British
Empire precisely was or was not *One Commonwealth*
in 1774, but I do venture to believe that John Adams's
view of this pivotal question of the American Revolution seems somewhat more consonant with all the
precedents I have been able to find than the opposing theory supported by Lord Mansfield in the eighteenth century, and now apparently held by a majority
of American historians.